Disorganized Attachment Detox

Regulate Your Emotions, Mend Past Wounds, Nurture Self-Worth, and Stop Fearful-Avoidant Patterns to Become Secure - Feel Safe & Build Trust in Relationships

A.J BROOKS

Copyright © 2024 by A.J BROOKS

All rights reserved.

No portion of this book may be reproduced in any form without written permission from the publisher or author, except as permitted by U.S. copyright law.This publication is designed to provide accurate and authoritative information in regard to the subject matter covered.

It is sold with the understanding that neither the author nor the publisher is engaged in rendering legal, investment, accounting or other professional services.

While the publisher and author have used their best efforts in preparing this book, they make no representations or warranties with respect to the accuracy or completeness of the contents of this book and specifically disclaim any implied warranties of merchantability or fitness for a particular purpose.

No warranty may be created or extended by sales representatives or written sales materials. The advice and strategies contained herein may not be suitable for your situation.

You should consult with a professional when appropriate. Neither the publisher nor the author shall be liable for any loss of profit or any other commercial damages, including but not limited to special, incidental, consequential, personal, or other damages.

Contents

Introduction	vii
1. UNDERSTANDING DISORGANIZED ATTACHMENT	1
The Basics of Attachment Theory	1
Decoding Disorganized Attachment: Traits and Triggers	3
The Neuroscience Behind Disorganized Attachment	5
How Early Experiences Shape Attachment Styles	7
The Spectrum of Attachment: From Secure to Disorganized	9
Recognizing Disorganized Behaviors in Daily Life	10
The Psychological Impact of Disorganized Attachment	12
2. EMOTIONAL REGULATION AND SELF-DISCOVERY	15
Strategies for Coping with Emotional Overwhelm	15
Building Emotional Intelligence: Tools and Exercises	17
Exploring the Influence of Mindfulness on Managing Emotions	19
Identifying and Expressing Your Emotional Needs	22
The Impact of Self-Compassion on Healing	24
Journaling for Emotional Clarity and Release	26
The Role of Meditation in Controlling Impulses	28
Strategies for Immediate Emotional Relief	30
3. NAVIGATING RELATIONSHIPS WITH DISORGANIZED ATTACHMENT	33
Exploring Intimacy Through the Lens of Attachment	33
Communication Skills for Healthier Relationships	35
The Impact of Disorganized Attachment on Romantic Partnerships	38
Strategies for Building Trust with Others	40

Co-regulation Techniques for Couples	42
Setting and Respecting Boundaries in Relationships	45
Managing Relationship Anxiety	46
Overcoming Impulse Actions in Relationships	49

4. FROM FEAR TO SECURITY: TRANSITIONING ATTACHMENT STYLES — 53

The Concept of Earned Secure Attachment	53
Ways to Foster Healthy Relationship Behaviors	55
Role Models and Mentoring in Developing Security	58
Overcoming the Fear of Abandonment	60
Embracing Vulnerability: Pathway to Secure Attachment	62
Reparenting Yourself Towards Security	64
Using Positive Psychology to Reinforce security	65
Breaking the Cycle of Seeking validation	67

5. HEALING FROM PAST TRAUMAS — 71

The Connection Between Trauma and Attachment Styles	71
Therapeutic Approaches to Healing Attachment Wounds	73
Integrating Body-Based Therapies for Trauma Release	76
The Role of EMDR in Resolving Attachment Issues	79
Creating a Personalized Healing Ritual	81
Support Systems and Their Role in Healing Trauma	83

6. PRACTICAL TOOLS FOR EVERYDAY CHALLENGES — 87

Navigating Social Interactions with Confidence	87
Dealing with Emotional Triggers in the Workplace	90
Techniques for Impulse Control	92
Avoiding Relationship Sabotage: Practical Tips	94
Self-Monitoring Tools for Attachment Behaviors	95
Using Technology to Support Attachment Health	98

7. ADVANCED STRATEGIES FOR RELATIONSHIP STABILITY — 101

Long-Term Relationship Planning with Disorganized Attachment	101
Advanced Co-regulation Strategies for Couples	103

Maintaining Emotional Balance in Family Dynamics	105
The Role of Forgiveness in Healing Relationships	107
Rebuilding Trust After Betrayal	110
Sustaining Improvements: Preventing Relapse into Old Patterns	112
8. THE IMPACT ON FAMILY AND PARENTING	**115**
Understanding Your Role in Family Attachment Patterns	115
Breaking the Cycle: Parenting with Awareness	118
Building Secure Attachments with Your Children	121
Healing Family Wounds	123
Supporting a Partner or Family Member with Disorganized Attachment	125
9. EMPOWERING TRANSFORMATION: YOUR PATH TO SECURE ATTACHMENT	**129**
Celebrating Small Wins on the Path to Security	129
Case Studies of Successful Attachment Transformations	131
Developing a Lifelong Attachment Health Plan	133
The Importance of Community and Support Networks	135
Embracing New Beginnings with Confidence and Hope	137
Life Beyond Fearful-Avoidant Attachment Patterns	139
Conclusion	143
References	147

Introduction

Have you ever found yourself going through ups and downs in your relationships, not romantically but also with friends, family, and even coworkers? Do you experience moments of closeness followed by distance, trust mixed with suspicion, or love intertwined with fear? If these emotions sound familiar to you, you may be feeling the impact of attachment.

Disorganized attachment often stems from a past where security and consistency were lacking. Simply put, this attachment style forms when inconsistencies and conflicting signals mark early relationships with caregivers. For individuals with this attachment pattern, relationships may seem like navigating a maze blindfolded – every step could lead to comfort or further confusion.

My journey mirrors yours. Some years back, I found myself in the midst of a storm in my own relationships. It was then that I had a profound realization. The patterns I kept repeating weren't random; they were deeply rooted in my early experiences. This insight, hard-earned through pain and deep reflection, marked the beginning of my journey toward understanding and healing. Since then, I've been dedicated to guiding others through this challenging terrain, drawing from both my personal experiences and extensive research.

In this book, I aim to help you understand and acquire the tools needed to move toward a secure attachment style. This book offers strategies based on the latest psychological research. It includes personal stories to support you on your journey of transformation.

This is not just another academic exploration of attachment theory. Here, we focus on the potential for healing. By engaging in practical exercises and gaining a compassionate understanding of your past, you can lay the groundwork for lasting security in your relationships. Each chapter is designed to shape your style progressively, empowering you to take control of your journey.

As you approach this book, I urge you not to see yourself as a mere reader but as an active participant in your journey of change. By embracing the exercises and insights with an open heart and mind, you can significantly impact your life. Remember, you are not alone on this path; many have walked it before you, and many will follow. Today is about taking that first step towards forming more stable and rewarding connections with yourself and others. I am here to guide you every step of the way.

I have faith in your ability to transform your relationships and discover joyous connections with the world around you. Let's embark on this adventure together, filled with optimism and a dedication to development. Welcome to the beginning of "Disorganized Attachment Detox." Let's kickstart the transformation process.

Chapter 1

Understanding Disorganized Attachment

As you flip through these pages, you might find yourself wrestling with emotions and patterns in your relationships that feel confusing and overwhelming at times. There are moments when intimacy can feel intimidating, and trust may appear hard to sustain. While these experiences can be quite challenging, they are not uncommon among individuals with disorganized attachment styles. This section aims to delve into the complexities of attachment theory, mainly focusing on the style to help shed light on the origins of these experiences and lay the groundwork for further enlightening insights.

The Basics of Attachment Theory

Attachment theory, initially studied by John Bowlby in the mid-20th century, offers a framework for understanding how our early interactions with caregivers shape our growth and social interactions significantly. Bowlby suggested that children have an inclination to form attachments with caregivers as a means of survival. Mary Ainsworth expanded on this idea through her research methodology, which aimed to observe different attachment styles in relationships. Together, these visionaries paved the way for comprehending how our initial connections impact our well-being and attachment behaviors across our lifespan.

Attachment styles – including secure, anxious, avoidant, and disorganized – delineate the dynamics of our relationships with those closest to us.

A strong and secure attachment style is characterized by a consistent bond with the caregiver, fostering relationships built on trust and emotional openness. On the other hand, anxious and avoidant attachments stem from inconsistent caregiving, resulting in relationships riddled with worry and emotional distance.

Disorganized attachment, the focus of our discussions, emerges from erratic caregiver responses and sometimes unsettling behaviors. This style is notable for lacking an approach to handling threats, leading to behaviors where both closeness and distance are both desired and feared.

The development of attachment behaviors can be interpreted as adaptive strategies that improve the chances of survival for our ancestors. For example, staying near a caregiver ensures protection and assistance for vulnerable young ones. Likewise, the idea of caregivers offering a haven during distress cements this bond by providing immediate solace and a foundation for exploring the world.

In psychology, recognizing one's attachment style is essential for self-awareness and navigating personal relationships. Tools like Ainsworth's Strange Situation Protocol or the Adult Attachment Interview enable researchers and clinicians to evaluate styles effectively.

These approaches include watching how a child behaves when separated from and reunited with their caregiver or interviewing adults about their childhood relationships to gain insights into their styles.

Reflective Question

Take a moment to reflect on your earliest relationships; How do you believe they might have shaped the way you currently interact with others? Ponder this query as we delve deeper into the intricacies of theory and its relevance in your life.

By grasping the basics of attachment theory, you are embarking on a journey to uncover the complexities of your relational dynamics. Armed with this knowledge, we can effectively navigate the challenges posed by disorganized attachment, paving the way for healing and personal growth in the chapters ahead.

Decoding Disorganized Attachment: Traits and Triggers

In the realm of disorganized attachment, the signals exchanged can often seem conflicting, leading to a web of relational uncertainty not only for those directly involved but also for those in their proximity. This sense of confusion primarily arises from the nature of their early bonds—where caregivers who should offer security instead vacillated between nurturing and threatening behaviors. These encounters instill a sense of puzzlement regarding intimacy; it is both desired and dreaded, pursued yet simultaneously avoided. This inner conflict holds weight; it profoundly shapes how adult relationships are approached.

Imagine someone with a disorganized attachment style who tends to seek comfort from their partner when feeling distressed. When offered support, they might react by pulling or even showing hostility. This back-and-forth dynamic can understandably create confusion and instability in their relationships.

Digging deeper, the root cause of these interactions often stems from the underlying feelings of fear and uncertainty associated with disorganized attachment. The unpredictability in caregiving experiences, where protection was inconsistent and sometimes frightening, instills a deep-seated doubt about the dependability of close relationships. Fear of abandonment or rejection plays a significant role in this dynamic. It drives the individual to seek connection for security while simultaneously pushing them to resist closeness as a defense mechanism against betrayal or pain. These conflicting emotions can result in behaviors that are hard for others to comprehend and for the individual themselves to articulate or recognize. It's not uncommon for such individuals to feel puzzled by their reactions; one moment, they crave closeness intensely, and the next, they feel an overwhelming urge to isolate themselves to avoid potential emotional harm.

Moreover, this disorganized pattern in relationships often mirrors unprocessed fears—unresolved traumas linked to caregivers who were both sources of comfort and sources of fear.

This lingering trauma can make a person feel constantly on edge, making it hard to form reliable connections with others. This leads to a life filled with ups and downs in relationships, where the longing for trust clashes with seated doubts. While these behaviors might seem erratic or unreasonable to outsiders, they are reactions stemming from ingrained fears of the person experiencing them.

Understanding these characteristics and triggers is vital not only for individuals with disorganized attachment styles but also for their partners, friends, and family members. It offers a framework for actions that might otherwise be misunderstood as irrational or harmful. Recognizing that these behaviors stem from a mix of past trauma and fear can foster empathy and assistance crucial for healing and personal development. It initiates conversations that go beyond blame and involve discussions about needs, boundaries, and recovery. In relationships, this insight can shift interactions from conflicts or misunderstandings towards stable engagements where both parties acknowledge deep-rooted fears and collaborate toward security and consistency.

The Neuroscience Behind Disorganized Attachment

When we delve into the complexities of disorganized attachment, we uncover the significant impact that brain function has on shaping our emotional responses and reactions to stress. Vital regions of the brain, such as the amygdala, hippocampus, and prefrontal cortex, play roles in managing emotions and how we interact with our surroundings, especially during our early developmental stages. The amygdala, known as the brain's alarm system, is crucial in processing fear and emotional memories. It tends to be overactive in individuals with disorganized attachment patterns, leading to increased vigilance and anxiety. This can elucidate why some people may overreact to perceived threats in relationships by sensing danger where others may not.

The hippocampus, which is in charge of memory processing and retrieval, also holds importance. In those with disorganized attachment styles, the hippocampus can be affected not only in its physical structure but also in its functioning. This can result in challenges differentiating between traumas and current situations. For instance, this could result in a flood of memories overwhelming an individual during a minor disagreement, making it difficult to remain rooted in the present moment. On the other hand, the prefrontal cortex – responsible for rational thinking and decision-making – typically works to regulate emotions triggered by the amygdala.

When it comes to disorganized attachment, where the ability to regulate emotions is compromised, making rational decisions during emotional situations can be quite challenging. Neuroimaging studies offer insights into how these dysfunctions present themselves. For example, individuals with disorganized attachment tendencies often exhibit different brain activity in response to emotional stimuli compared to those with secure attachment styles. This neural evidence is significant as it connects the behavioral aspects of disorganized attachment directly to observable brain function, providing a biological perspective on the daily experiences of those affected.

The impact of trauma goes beyond just affecting these essential brain regions' development. Childhood adversities such as caregiving or exposure to fear-inducing situations can result in lasting alterations in brain structure and function. This is particularly noticeable in how the brain handles stress and trauma. For instance, ongoing stress can heighten the amygdala's sensitivity to threats, leading individuals to be more alert in seemingly safe environments. At the time, this stress can impede the growth and functioning of the hippocampus, making it challenging to form coherent memories chronologically and potentially resulting in fragmented or disorganized recollections.

However, there is a flicker of optimism in the brain's ability to adapt, known as neuroplasticity. This term refers to the brain's capability to restructure itself by forming neural connections throughout a person's lifespan. This capacity plays a role in recovering from trauma and cultivating healthier attachment patterns. Therapeutic methods that involve positive new attachment experiences and support can activate neuroplasticity, encouraging the development of more adaptive neural pathways. Treatments that concentrate on managing emotions, processing trauma, and fostering relational interactions can physically alter how the brain responds to the environment. This restructuring goes beyond calming an overly active amygdala or enhancing the rational functions of the prefrontal cortex; it involves nurturing a harmonized brain that promotes feelings of safety and connection in relationships.

Understanding the neuroscience underpinning attachment not only demystifies many perplexing experiences and reactions linked with this style but also highlights the potential for profound change. This knowledge equips us with a foundation for hope—a hope rooted in our brain's biology—which confirms that recovery and transformation are achievable through comprehension and empathetic intervention.

As we delve deeper into the concept of attachment, it's essential to remember that every bit of insight contributes to a better understanding of not only the obstacles but also the ways to achieve healing and balance.

How Early Experiences Shape Attachment Styles

How our initial interactions with caregivers shape our attachment styles is crucial for understanding how we navigate relationships in adulthood. The way a caregiver responds to an infant, whether nurturing or unpredictable, lays the foundation for how that child will perceive and engage with the world as they grow older. Based on the theories of Ainsworth and Bowlby, it becomes clear just how significant these early experiences are. Ainsworth's Strange Situation procedure highlighted the impact of responsive versus caregiving on children's behavior. At the same time, Bowlby's theory underlined how attachment quality in early life could influence relationships later on.

These early encounters essentially set the stage for our beliefs about relationship dynamics. For example, consistent and caring caregiving promotes an attachment style where individuals feel secure and valued in their connections with others. Conversely, erratic or absent caregiver behavior can lead to a disorganized attachment style. Children exposed to this type of caregiving may experience signals—pushed away when seeking comfort but pulled close when asserting independence.

The puzzling nature of experiences often leaves individuals without a clear plan to build strong relationships, leading them to carry this turbulent relational model into their adult lives.

Research has extensively documented the lasting impact of these interactions, showing that early attachment experiences can significantly influence future emotional and social outcomes. For instance, individuals who have experienced disorganized attachment in the past are more likely to struggle with maintaining stable relationships and may also be at a higher risk for various psychological challenges like anxiety and depression. These findings emphasize the role of early attachment experiences in shaping an individual's life path over time.

Furthermore, the delicate balance between tendencies and environmental circumstances during the formative years of childhood is essential for establishing attachments. Although genetics may predispose a child to traits or behaviors, the interactions with caregivers during this critical period profoundly impact attachment styles. This dynamic relationship suggests that while innate characteristics exist, our upbringing significantly influences how we learn to connect with others and regulate our emotions.

Given the rooted impact of early experiences on attachment formation, it is imperative to implement preventive measures that offer support to families at risk.

Providing intervention programs that offer guidance and education to parents on effective caregiving practices can have a significant impact. Initiatives that teach caregivers how to respond to their infants' needs or provide therapeutic assistance to parents dealing with disorganized attachment-related challenges have shown promising outcomes in promoting secure attachment patterns in children. These interventions not only help decrease disorganized attachment occurrences but also enhance the emotional and psychological well-being of both children and their caregivers.

Understanding these principles allows us to grasp the intricacies of attachment theory and its implications for our relationships and emotional well-being. As we delve deeper into these concepts, we not only gain insights into our behaviors and tendencies but also acquire strategies to reshape and mend our connections with others.

The Spectrum of Attachment: From Secure to Disorganized

Exploring the spectrum of attachment from secure to disorganized can be highly enlightening, offering insights into the reasons behind our behavior in relationships. This spectrum comprises anxious, avoidant, and disorganized attachment styles, each with unique characteristics and approaches to interacting with others. A secure attachment style is characterized by confidence in the availability and support of loved ones, fostering more harmonious relationships.

People with anxious attachment tend to worry a lot about their relationships, desiring closeness but also fearing being abandoned. On the other hand, individuals with avoidant attachment feel uneasy about getting too close to others and often keep their emotions at a distance. Disorganized attachment combines elements of both avoidant and anxious attachment styles. Still, it shows greater inconsistency due to conflicting experiences with caregivers in early life. Unlike the predictable behaviors of anxious or avoidant attachment styles, disorganized attachment is characterized by unpredictable actions and mixed signals. This can be confusing for both the person with disorganized attachment and those around them. While those with an anxious attachment style may seek reassurance consistently, a person with a disorganized attachment might switch between seeking closeness one moment and reacting fearfully or withdrawing the next without clear reasons. This unpredictability can make relationships turbulent and difficult to navigate.

Moving along this range, especially transitioning from a state of disorganized to secure attachment, is definitely achievable. It is often supported by significant life changes or therapeutic interventions. Therapy offers a stable relational experience that can assist in reshaping attachment patterns. Major life events like entering into a relationship, becoming a parent, or facing loss can also act as triggers for transformation. These occurrences may prompt individuals to reflect on their behaviors and actively seek change.

To illustrate these ideas visually, imagine a diagram that places each style on a spectrum. At one end lies secure attachment, which is characterized by high self-esteem and comfort with intimacy. Progressing along the spectrum reveals avoidant attachments that show increasing insecurity, discomfort with intimacy, and heightened self-centeredness. Disorganized attachment resides at the end, marked by high levels of anxiety and avoidance, indicating the complexity and seriousness of this style. This visual representation aids in understanding how these styles interconnect and their impact on aspects of life such as relationship satisfaction, personal development, and emotional well-being.

The process of recognizing and reshaping one's style is deeply personal and can pose challenges. However, the insights gained through this exploration can be incredibly freeing.

Mapping our position on this spectrum and grasping the essence of our connections allows us to nurture stronger relationships and personal development. This fundamental understanding acts as a bridge to self-discovery and more rewarding interactions with the people in our lives. While delving into the complexities of attachment and its evolution, remember the significance of empathy and comprehension in facilitating growth and recovery.

Recognizing Disorganized Behaviors in Daily Life

Disorganized attachment can manifest in subtle yet profound ways in our daily interactions and choices, often leaving us puzzled about our responses and the complexity of our feelings. Recognizing these behaviors marks the step towards comprehending and handling disorganized attachment more effectively. One common characteristic is the struggle to make decisions, especially when they involve risks or relational outcomes. This uncertainty often originates from the fear of making a decision that could result in abandonment or conflict, reflecting the instability and unpredictability encountered in early attachments.

Picture a situation where someone with disorganized attachment must choose between committing to a serious relationship or pursuing a more casual connection. The decision-making process can become a source of anxiety and uncertainty. On one side, there is a desire for close and secure bonds, while on the other hand, there is a profound fear of getting too close, which could lead to pain or loss. This internal conflict may not be apparent to others, causing the individual's actions to seem erratic or unexplained.

In work environments, particularly those with high-stress levels, individuals with disorganized attachments may suddenly retreat from social interactions or display inconsistent levels of participation.

During projects, individuals may start off by actively participating out of a desire to connect and be part of the team. However, as the project advances, the fear of criticism or failure could lead to a retreat, leaving colleagues puzzled by the shift in behavior. This trend not only impacts one's professional relationships but also influences one's career growth and self-confidence.

For those grappling with disorganized attachment patterns in their loved ones, knowing how to respond supportively to these behaviors is crucial. It entails creating an environment where open discussions about fears and needs can take place without judgment. For instance, if a loved one withdraws unexpectedly, addressing the behavior with compassion can make a difference. A simple acknowledgment such as "I've noticed you've been quiet lately. Is there something on your mind that you'd like to share?" can pave the way for conversations and reassurance.

Additionally, mastering self-awareness techniques is vital for individuals working on managing traits associated with disorganized attachment. One effective strategy involves keeping a journal of behaviors.

By documenting instances of confusion, hesitation, withdrawal, or similar behaviors in this journal, it becomes easier to recognize patterns and triggers.

Over time, keeping a journal can become a tool for recognizing specific situations or interactions that may worsen disorganized behaviors. This helps in being better prepared and having response strategies in place. For instance, if someone consistently writes about feeling anxious during family gatherings in their journal, it could indicate a connection to family dynamics as a trigger. Being able to identify this pattern enables the individual to develop coping mechanisms like setting boundaries for attending events or mentally preparing beforehand. Taking these measures is crucial for enhancing emotional stability and fostering better relationships with others.

By addressing and reflecting on these behaviors, individuals experiencing disorganized attachment patterns can start seeing improvements in their daily interactions. Engaging in this practice of self-awareness and emotional regulation not only promotes personal development but also plays a significant role in achieving more stable and fulfilling relationships. It's important to remember that every small step taken towards understanding and managing these behaviors contributes to a journey towards healthier connections with the world and those around us.

The Psychological Impact of Disorganized Attachment

Living with a disorganized attachment style often involves dealing with various emotional hurdles that arise from underlying challenges and practicing self-regulation.

The challenge of managing emotions can impact various aspects of life, significantly affecting relationships and job stability. For example, let's think about how emotions can run in a typical work conflict.

While some people handle these situations calmly, those with issues may struggle, swinging between anger and withdrawal without fully understanding why. This rollercoaster of emotions can strain work relationships. This leads to an inconsistent job history since workplaces value consistent emotional responses.

Additionally, difficulties in controlling emotions are linked to a risk of mental health problems. Studies show that individuals with disorders, including disorganized attachment, are more prone to developing anxiety, depression, and PTSD. The unpredictability of emotions can contribute to psychological distress and make it hard to find emotional balance. This instability can worsen existing health issues or trigger new ones, creating a challenging cycle that may require professional help to break.

For instance, the ongoing worry caused by disorganized attachment can increase the likelihood of developing generalized anxiety disorder, where a person experiences constant worry and tension that goes beyond normal reactions to daily stressors. This also impacts interactions. Those dealing with disorganized attachment often struggle in social situations due to fear and mistrust stemming from unpredictable early life experiences. This can lead to behaviors that isolate them or create conflicts with others. Some may avoid interactions out of fear of rejection, while others may misinterpret social cues and expect hostility or abandonment, leading to strained relationships. These challenges highlight the importance of individuals coping with disorganized attachment and developing strategies to manage their emotions effectively. Simple techniques such as breathing exercises, mindfulness meditation, and regular physical activity can help regulate emotions and improve emotional control.

For example, applying mindfulness meditation can help individuals become more aware of the moment and better handle overwhelming emotions instead of being overwhelmed by them.

Another method is keeping a journal. By recording their feelings, triggers, and responses, people can gain insights into recurring patterns that may be contributing to their challenges. This ongoing introspection can be valuable for understanding and dealing with the effects of disorganized attachment. It involves engaging in an inner dialogue that gradually shifts from confusion and disorder to clarity and organization.

These coping mechanisms serve as a starting point. As we delve into in-depth strategies in the upcoming sections, it's important to remember that each step taken brings us closer to grasping, managing, and ultimately transforming disorganized attachment patterns into more secure and stable ways of engaging with the world. Every effort counts, no matter how small, in crafting a tapestry of emotional strength and social cohesion.

Chapter 2

Emotional Regulation and Self-Discovery

Exploring the journey of self-discovery and managing your emotions can sometimes feel like navigating through a vast ocean. Every emotional wave, whether intense or not, requires your attention and respect. For individuals experiencing disorganized attachment, these waves may appear daunting, unpredictable, and isolating at times. However, envision possessing a compass and tools that not only assist you in riding these waves but also guide you in navigating through them confidently and resiliently. This section aims to equip you with these tools to better handle overwhelm, leading you towards calmer waters of emotional stability and deeper self-awareness.

Strategies for Coping with Emotional Overwhelm

Being able to identify signs of emotional overwhelm is essential in preventing stress from escalating into uncontrolled reactions that are often regrettable. Signs like a racing heart rate, irritability, or overwhelming panic serve as alarms from your body, indicating turbulent emotional conditions where proactive steps are necessary. Recognizing these signs without criticism is the first step in regaining control over your emotional well-being.

During turbulent times, grounding techniques act as stabilizing anchors to help navigate the stormy seas of emotions.

Here are some practical and simple strategies that can help you find balance. One helpful technique is mindful breathing, where you take slow, deep breaths to calm your body's stress response. By focusing on each breath, you can bring a sense of peace. Redirect your attention from overwhelming emotions. Another effective way to ground yourself is through activities such as holding ice, feeling different textures, or enjoying scents. These sensory experiences can shift your focus away from distress. Offer immediate relief by bringing you back to the present moment.

Developing a safety plan is like mapping out a journey before embarking on it. This plan involves understanding what triggers your stress, preparing responses for those triggers, and listing resources or people you can turn to when needed. Begin by recognizing situations that have caused stress in the past. Then, outline practical steps to follow when faced with circumstances again. This could involve stepping from a stressful situation using grounding techniques or reaching out to a supportive individual.

Having a well-thought-out strategy is akin to having a reliable map in hand; it gives a sense of security and readiness that can significantly help in handling disorganized attachments.

In today's world, technology plays a major role in supporting emotional well-being. Various applications and gadgets are created to assist in monitoring stress levels and recommending solutions for effective stress management. For example, wearable devices can monitor signals like heart rate and body temperature, which serve as indicators of stress. Applications can offer guided breathing exercises, mindfulness practices, or brief meditation sessions customized to your condition. Using these resources can enable you to manage your emotions efficiently, granting you a feeling of command and proficiency over your reactions.

Emotional Safety Plan Template

To help you develop your emotional safety plan, here's a simple template you can use:

1. *Identify Triggers:* List situations, people, or emotions that trigger your overwhelm.
2. *Plan Your Responses:* For each trigger, write down a specific action you will take to alleviate stress.
3. *List Your Go-To Resources:* Include contact information for friends, therapists, or hotlines you can reach out to when needed.
4. *Practice Regularly:* Regularly review and practice your plan to make your responses more automatic and effective.

By incorporating these techniques and tools into your routine, you not only improve your ability to handle overwhelming emotions but also take important steps in your journey towards emotional regulation and self-discovery. Each action boosts your confidence and skills, preparing you to navigate the challenges of a disorganized attachment style with greater ease and resilience. As you keep exploring and implementing these strategies, remember that each moment of practice brings you closer to a stable and rewarding emotional life.

Building Emotional Intelligence: Tools and Exercises

Emotional intelligence (EI) is an aspect of personal growth, especially when dealing with the nuances of disorganized attachment. At its core, EI consists of five elements: self-awareness, self-regulation, motivation, empathy, and social skills. Each of these elements plays a role in understanding and handling your own emotions as well as those of people around you. Self-awareness helps you identify your emotions and the triggers that could disrupt your equilibrium. Self-regulation enables you to manage those emotions effectively without letting them dictate your behavior. Motivation involves using your emotions to pursue your goals.

Understanding and connecting with the emotions of others through empathy can strengthen relationships and create deeper bonds. Social experiences nurture communication and interaction skills, which are crucial in various aspects of life.

The initial step in developing an Emotional Intelligence (EI) is enhancing self-awareness, especially for individuals dealing with disorganized attachment where emotions may seem complex. Engaging in practices like tracking moods can offer valuable insights. By recording emotions and their triggers, one can identify patterns in emotional responses. This not only helps recognize triggers but also aids in devising effective coping strategies. Delving deeper into self-awareness through questions such as "What emotion did I experience most intensely today and why?" or "In which situations did I feel secure or insecure?" facilitates a thorough exploration of one's emotional landscape, fostering a better understanding of feelings and reactions.

Another aspect of EI, building empathy, goes beyond comprehending others' emotions; it involves empathizing with them genuinely. This may pose a challenge for individuals who have learned to shield their feelings due to experiencing insecure attachment behaviors.

Engaging with literature and art that stir emotions can serve as a gentle way to start embracing empathy. By immersing yourself in the experiences of characters or the expressive nature of art, you begin to connect with universal sentiments like happiness, sadness, love, and grief. This helps bridge the gap between your feelings and those of others. Role-playing scenarios also prove effective in this regard. Stepping into another person's shoes in a simulated setting allows you to practice understanding and responding to emotions in a manner that fosters connections rather than conflicts.

Enhancing awareness skills is crucial for anyone seeking to boost their Emotional Intelligence (EI), as these skills directly influence the quality of interactions and relationships. Active listening stands out as one skill that can revolutionize your communication approach. It entails focusing on the speaker comprehending their message, responding thoughtfully, and recalling the information later on. This not only demonstrates respect for the speaker but also enhances your capacity to comprehend and connect with them on a deeper level. Moreover, mastering verbal communication cues—such as maintaining eye contact, interpreting body language, and being mindful of your facial expressions—can greatly improve your ability to analyze and respond effectively in social settings.

These signals often convey more than words and can offer deeper insights into the feelings and motives of others. By incorporating these practices into your routine, you improve your emotional intelligence, gradually arming yourself with the necessary skills to handle chaotic attachment styles more efficiently and cultivate more meaningful relationships. Keep in mind that each effort you put into enhancing your EI leads to opportunities for self-improvement and meaningful connections, creating a path towards a life where emotions are not merely experienced but comprehended and handled with care and understanding.

Exploring the Influence of Mindfulness on Managing Emotions

Picture yourself in a setting next to a calm lake, watching the gentle ripples on its surface. Each ripple symbolizes a passing thought, emotion, or sensation in your mind. Mindfulness encourages you to observe these ripples without passing judgment to comprehend their origins and to release them without disrupting your peace. This ancient practice, rooted in beliefs, has become an essential tool in contemporary psychological approaches, especially concerning emotional regulation and repairing attachment styles.

Mindfulness revolves around being engaged in the present moment, conscious of our thoughts, emotions, and sensations without feeling overwhelmed by them. For individuals navigating the waters of disorganized attachment styles, mindfulness provides a means to steady the mind and cultivate a sense of security within oneself. It assists in identifying and pausing reactions that often govern behavior during stressful encounters. Through practicing mindfulness, one can develop the ability to respond to situations with clarity and avoid reacting out of fear or past experiences.

The advantages of mindfulness are not just theoretical. Are supported by extensive research findings. Research indicates that regular mindfulness exercises can notably help you manage symptoms related to anxiety, depression, and stress.

Enhancing resilience can help you better navigate life's challenges. For individuals with attachment issues, improving emotional regulation can be incredibly beneficial. This process creates a buffer between emotions and actions, giving you the space to choose how to respond in a way that nurtures your well-being and relationships.

Mindfulness can be developed through meditation techniques, each serving a unique purpose. For instance, focused attention meditation involves concentrating on a focal point like your breath or a flickering candle flame. This practice boosts your ability to regain composure when emotions run high. On the other hand, open-monitoring meditation promotes broader awareness by observing all aspects of your experiences without attachment. This type of meditation is particularly useful for understanding your thought patterns and behaviors linked to attachment styles.

Incorporating mindfulness into your life is more straightforward than you might imagine. It begins with meaningful practices such as mindful eating, where you savor each bite, paying attention to flavors, textures, and sensations.

You could also experiment with walking, focusing entirely on the sensation of walking, feeling the ground under your feet and the gentle breeze on your skin. These practices help train your mind to be present and attentive, reducing the risk of feeling overwhelmed by your thoughts or feelings.

A growing body of scientific evidence backs the benefits of mindfulness for enhancing emotional well-being. Studies in neuroscience, for instance, demonstrate that mindfulness meditation can bring about changes in brain regions associated with focus, emotional control, and self-awareness. These changes not only boost your ability to cope with stress but also enhance your overall mental health. Through engagement in mindfulness exercises, you essentially rewire your brain to better handle emotional challenges, fostering a greater sense of emotional stability and assurance.

Integrating mindfulness into your life doesn't necessitate a complete overhaul of your schedule or significant time investment. It begins with a commitment to pause, breathe, and observe your world with curiosity and kindness. As you become more adept at these practices, you'll likely observe a transformation in how you engage with your thoughts and feelings. They cease to dominate you; instead, you acquire the tools and clarity to navigate them gracefully and accurately.

This significant change is transformative, providing a way to move beyond the confusion of disorganized attachment and towards a more balanced, secure existence. As you delve deeper into your thoughts, remember that each moment of mindfulness takes you closer to a calmer, grounded version of yourself capable of building stronger, more enriching connections.

Identifying and Expressing Your Emotional Needs

Recognizing and communicating your requirements is like having the right tools in a toolbox; without this awareness, addressing any challenge would be much harder. Emotional needs are desires that, when fulfilled, enable you to thrive and feel content in your relationships. These needs can vary from seeking acceptance and affection to safety and empathy. It's vital to differentiate these from desires—such as wanting a specific gift or outcome in social situations. While wants may bring joy meeting emotional needs is essential for lasting happiness and security.

Identifying your emotional needs involves self-reflection and introspection. It calls for looking within yourself and examining what emotions consistently arise when you feel uneasy or dissatisfied in your relationships.

When you often feel nervous or uneasy during your interactions with others, it could mean that you have a desire for safety and stability that is not being fulfilled. Understanding these needs is the step in dealing with them. It enables you to communicate clearly and to look for environments and relationships that support your well-being.

The significance of needs in relationships cannot be emphasized enough. When you know your needs, you are better able to express them effectively to others, reducing misunderstandings and conflicts. Furthermore, when partners can openly share their needs in a relationship, it creates an atmosphere of respect and understanding. This openness is not limited to relationships but extends to friendships, family dynamics, and professional relationships as well. By articulating your needs, you encourage others to grasp your perspective deeply, leading to more supportive and fulfilling interactions.

Effectively communicating your needs requires skills and approaches that promote clarity and prevent discord. One such approach is using "I" statements. This method involves framing your thoughts in a way that focuses on your emotions rather than assigning blame or criticism to someone else.

When you say, "I feel like my input is being overlooked" or "You never consider what I have to say, "it can change how your message is perceived and lead to better outcomes. This approach helps reduce defensiveness and increases the chances of your needs being understood and respected.

Nonviolent communication (NVC) is another tool that emphasizes expressing needs without aggression. Developed by Marshall Rosenberg, NVC involves a four-step process:

- Observing without judgment
- Sharing feelings
- Identifying needs
- Making requests

This method promotes empathy and constructive dialogue by focusing on needs rather than surface conflicts.

Let's consider Maria's case to demonstrate the effectiveness of these strategies. Maria, a client struggling with feeling valued in her relationships, discovered through therapy that she needed to be heard and respected to feel secure. By using "I" statements to communicate her needs with her partner, she gradually gained confidence despite challenges. Over time, her partner learned to listen and create space for her contributions.

Over time, the new way they communicated changed their relationship, creating an equal and satisfying dynamic for both of them. As you delve into your world and discover how to express your needs effectively, remember that each step you take enhances your connections and enriches your interactions. By being aware of and articulating what you require, you open up opportunities for more meaningful relationships that are congruent with your core desires and values.

The Impact of Self-Compassion on Healing

In the realm of growth and emotional well-being, self-compassion shines as a gentle yet potent guiding light. Initially introduced by Dr. Kristin Neff, self-compassion is a practice centered on treating yourself with the same kindness, care, and support as you would give to a close friend. At its essence, self-compassion consists of three aspects: kindness, shared humanity, and mindfulness. Embracing and nurturing these components can significantly shift how you perceive yourself and engage with the world—especially when navigating the emotions tied to disorganized attachment.

Self-kindness in this context involves being compassionate and empathetic toward oneself without resorting to harsh criticism or judgment.

Instead of being too hard on yourself for your flaws, showing self-compassion encourages you to treat yourself with kindness and understanding. Recognizing that everyone experiences suffering and feelings of inadequacy as part of our shared journey rather than feeling like it's just happening to you alone, this perspective helps you feel more connected in your struggles. Being means finding a balanced way to deal with negative emotions without suppressing them or blowing them out of proportion. Developing this awareness through mindfulness is essential for maintaining a compassionate outlook.

One helpful method for cultivating self-compassion is writing letters to yourself. In these letters, you can speak to yourself in an understanding tone, reflecting on moments where you may have felt like you fell short or weren't "good enough." By expressing empathy, kindness, and acceptance towards yourself for these perceived shortcomings, this practice can be incredibly therapeutic. It can transform your dialogue from being critical to compassionate and nurture a more caring relationship with yourself.

Engaging in self-affirmations focused on self-kindness is another beneficial practice. These are affirming statements about yourself that you repeat regularly to reinforce your perceptions of yourself.

Embracing affirmations like "I am giving my best effort, and that's sufficient" or "I fully accept myself" can help shift negative narratives often linked to disorganized attachment. Building self-compassion not only impacts how you build and sustain relationships but also helps those with disorganized attachments navigate through insecurities and fears rooted in feelings of unworthiness. As self-compassion grows, it fosters a stable inner core, reducing the need for external validation and approval in relationships. This transformation can lead to more balanced connections where emotional well-being comes from within rather than relying solely on external validations.

However, developing self-compassion is a journey that many struggle with due to deep-rooted feelings of unworthiness. Overcoming the belief of being undeserving of kindness involves acknowledging these emotions as part of the shared experience tied to self-compassion. It's important to recognize that everyone faces moments of inadequacy at some point in their lives. By recognizing this human experience, you can start to view your own feelings of inadequacy as part of a larger shared experience rather than something unique to you alone. It can also be beneficial to challenge these negative beliefs, perhaps by using cognitive behavioral methods that help identify and counter irrational thoughts. Another approach could involve gradually engaging in acts of self-compassion, beginning with gestures like treating yourself to a peaceful bath or making time for a hobby you enjoy. As you integrate these practices into your routine, remember that each step towards self-kindness contributes to a more stable and satisfying emotional well-being. Embracing self-compassion not only improves your relationship with yourself but also has a positive impact on how you connect with others, fostering deeper relationships and promoting compassion in the world.

Journaling for Emotional Clarity and Release

Writing in a journal is like finding your way through a forest. It helps clear your mind and navigate your emotions with more clarity. For those dealing with feelings, journaling is a valuable tool for understanding emotions, sorting out thoughts, and ultimately reducing stress. When you put your thoughts on paper, you're not just jotting down events; you're engaging in a practice that promotes self-discovery and emotional healing.

Think of each journal entry as a piece of the puzzle that makes up your subconscious mind. Over time, these pieces can help you see the picture of your emotional world by uncovering patterns, triggers, and hidden truths about how you connect with others. This process of reflection is valuable because it lets you pinpoint what exactly causes discomfort or joy in your interactions or thoughts. It's like holding up a mirror to yourself and observing without feeling pressured to react or judge immediately. This can greatly reduce stress by creating a space where you can deal with emotions at your own pace, preventing overwhelming feelings during tense situations or triggering moments.

In this exercise, think about using specific journal prompts to explore your attachment issues, past traumas, and daily emotions. For example, you could write about a situation that sparked a strong emotional reaction. Describe what was said, how it made you feel, and why you believe it impacted you deeply. Another prompt might prompt you to reminisce about a childhood memory that shapes your perspective on relationships. These prompts encourage exploration of your emotional landscape and shed light on how past experiences shape your present attachment patterns.

Setting up an environment for journaling is just as crucial as the act itself. Choose a comfortable space where you feel safe and relaxed. It could be a corner at home with soft lighting and a comfortable chair or a peaceful spot in nature where tranquility surrounds you. Privacy is key to freeing yourself from worries about judgment and allowing your thoughts to flow naturally. Personalize this space with items like plants or artwork that signal to your mind that it's a place for emotional introspection.

Consistency in journaling is vital for its effectiveness in regulation.

Make sure to allocate time each day or week for this practice, treating it with the same priority as any other appointment or commitment. Consistency will help to establish a routine and reinforce the habit of self-reflection and self-care. As time goes by, this regular journaling practice will become a cornerstone of your well-being, a safe haven where clarity and emotional release await.

Sample Journal Entry

Here's an example of a journal entry from someone dealing with their insecure attachment patterns:

"Today was quite challenging. In a work meeting, I suddenly felt overlooked when my suggestion was ignored. My heart dropped. I struggled to concentrate for the rest of the session. Looking back now, I realize that this triggered my fear of not feeling valued, a sentiment rooted in my childhood experiences of being sidelined within my family dynamics. Recognizing this brings forth both sadness for the version of myself who felt inadequate and relief in comprehending how this past pain influences my present relationship fears. Moving ahead, I aim to express my emotions in time, starting with less intimidating situations."

This entry showcases the revelations that can be uncovered through journaling.

It not only brings attention to immediate emotional responses but also links them to underlying historical emotions, giving a clearer view of the inner narrative that often motivates disorganized attachment behaviors.

The Role of Meditation in Controlling Impulses

The significance of meditation in controlling impulses is emphasized when dealing with attachment, where impulsive reactions can dominate, leading to regrettable situations. In this context, meditation is more than a routine; it serves as a refuge, equipping individuals with the means to comprehend and manage these impulses with heightened awareness and restraint. While mindfulness—embracing the moment with acceptance—is pivotal for emotional regulation, meditation takes it further by offering dedicated time for fostering awareness, focus, and emotional equilibrium.

Meditation differs from mindfulness as it entails setting aside periods for practicing techniques that enhance concentration and thought control. This deliberate practice surpasses the awareness cultivated by mindfulness, enabling individuals to explore their mental and emotional processes more deeply. Through meditation, individuals train their minds to concentrate on a point—such as their breath, a mantra, or a visual stimulus—which aids in handling the often overwhelming influx of thoughts and feelings associated with disorganized attachment.

One effective way to improve control through meditation is by practicing focused attention meditation. This method involves selecting a point and consistently redirecting your focus back to it whenever your mind starts to wander. For instance, you can simply concentrate on your breathing – paying attention to the inhalation and exhalation, the movement of your chest, or the feeling of air flowing through your nostrils. Whenever you notice your thoughts drifting elsewhere, gently guide them back to your breath. This practice helps enhance concentration skills and reduces reactions by training your mind to regain a sense of calm focus even in challenging situations.

Another beneficial technique is visualization meditation, where you visualize a place that brings about feelings of tranquility and relaxation. Picture yourself in a serene setting such as a beach, a lush forest, or a cozy sanctuary that resonates with you. Imagine the sights, sounds, smells, and textures of this place in detail. Engaging your senses in this way helps divert impulses and shifts your emotional state towards peace and steadiness. Visualization not only calms the mind but also enables you to create mental oases of safety, which can be especially valuable during times of chaos and unpredictability.

The connection between meditation practice and better emotional regulation is backed by numerous studies that demonstrate how meditation can boost the brain's ability to manage emotions and handle stress. This is because of neuroplasticity, which allows the brain to reorganize itself by creating new neural connections in response to learning or experiences. Meditation strengthens parts of the brain for self-control, like the prefrontal cortex, while decreasing activity in areas such as the amygdala linked to fear and emotional reactions. These changes not only aid in managing impulses but also promote a more thoughtful, less reactive approach to situations that may have previously triggered automatic or disorganized responses.

Consistency in practicing meditation is crucial for reaping these benefits. Starting with sessions of five to ten minutes can help make meditation more accessible and less intimidating. With time and experience, you can gradually increase the duration of your practice as you feel more at ease and can observe its effects. The goal is to incorporate meditation into your routine in a way that feels sustainable and fulfilling. Remember, perfection in meditation isn't necessary; instead, use it as a tool to cultivate emotional balance and resilience.

Making meditation a part of your life provides a meaningful way to gain control over impulsive behaviors stemming from disorganized attachment issues.

As you progress in your meditation journey, you might notice a shift in how you handle life's obstacles with peace and clarity. This change not only enhances your own well-being but also enhances your connections with others, leading to more stable and harmonious relationships. Therefore, as you move ahead, view meditation not as a routine but as a dedication to fostering a more balanced, composed, and emotionally stable self.

Strategies for Immediate Emotional Relief

During times when chaotic emotions seem overwhelming, having quick calming strategies on hand can be incredibly helpful. These techniques are meant to offer relief during periods of high stress or emotional overwhelm, providing temporary solutions that help stabilize your feelings until you can address the root causes more thoroughly. For example, practicing breathing is a straightforward yet highly effective way to center yourself. By focusing on deep breaths, you activate the parasympathetic nervous system, which helps to counteract automatic stress responses and promotes a sense of tranquility. Additionally, pausing to count to ten before reacting can offer a moment of reflection to avoid impulsive responses driven by intense emotions.

Engaging in tactile grounding exercises, such as holding onto a textured item such as a stone or stress ball, can be beneficial. These exercises provide an anchor to the present moment, diverting your attention from troubling thoughts or overwhelming emotions.

Understanding the science behind these calming methods can enhance their effectiveness. When under stress, your body triggers the nervous system, releasing stress hormones known as cortisol and adrenaline. These hormones prepare your body for fight or flight reactions, resulting in increased heart rate, breathing, and heightened muscle readiness – all useful for physical action but less so for emotional threats. Techniques like breathing counteract these changes by activating the parasympathetic nervous system, known as the "rest and digest" system. This helps the heart rate relax muscles and reduce blood pressure to aid in recovering from emotional spikes more quickly.

Imagine yourself in a work meeting with conflicting opinions or in a social situation where conversations unexpectedly trigger deep-rooted insecurities. In these instances, using quick calming techniques can be the key to responding calmly rather than reacting impulsively.

For instance, if you feel self-conscious during a meeting, taking a moment to breathe can help you handle your initial emotional reaction. This can enable you to respond with consideration rather than defensiveness. Likewise, if a social situation becomes too much to handle, stepping away for a walk while focusing on the sensation of the ground beneath your feet can help restore your emotional balance.

Developing a routine of using these strategies during stressful moments is important. Regular practice ingrains them into your natural response system, making them more intuitive over time. Mindfulness can further enhance this habit formation by heightening your awareness of your emotions and triggers. By practicing mindfulness, you become better at recognizing signs of stress or emotional overwhelm early on, enabling you to employ calming techniques more efficiently and promptly. Dedicate a few minutes each day to practicing these methods regardless of how you feel emotionally; this will solidify their place in your emotional toolkit so that they come naturally when needed most.

By incorporating these relief techniques into your daily life, you'll discover that they not only alleviate momentary challenges but also contribute to a greater sense of mastery over your emotions and responses. This newfound sense of stability is truly invaluable as you journey through the complexities of insecure attachment styles. It helps you stay grounded in the midst of emotional times.

As we conclude this section on managing emotions and self-exploration, we have explored approaches—ranging from recognizing and expressing your emotional needs to embracing the benefits of mindfulness and meditation. Each method brings its advantages, and when used together, they can significantly improve your ability to handle the emotional hurdles that come with disorganized attachment. Remember that every skill you've gained here serves as a building block towards achieving emotional clarity and resilience and ultimately forming more secure and fulfilling connections with yourself and others. Let these tools be your compass as you move forward to the stage where we will discuss navigating relationships impacted by disorganized attachment.

Chapter 3

Navigating Relationships with Disorganized Attachment

For individuals dealing with disorganized attachment, getting into or maintaining relationships can often feel like embarking on an unpredictable journey through a wild terrain where closeness seems both intimidating and appealing. What if there was a way to traverse this path with confidence and insight? This chapter is here to help, serving as your companion in delving into the depths of intimacy through the perspective of theory and presenting techniques to foster healthier and more rewarding connections.

Exploring Intimacy Through the Lens of Attachment

Intimacy, in its true essence, is about deeply knowing and being known by another person, whether in friendship, family, or romantic relationships. For those struggling with disorganized attachment patterns, intimacy tends to stir up conflicts and uncertainties. The core issue lies in the nature of attachment itself—stemming from inconsistent caregiving that mixed fear with comfort during early development, resulting in lingering doubts about forming close bonds.

This sense of uncertainty gives rise to an inner struggle regarding intimacy: the fear of getting too close (which makes one vulnerable to pain) and the fear of staying too distant (which leads to feelings of loneliness), making it difficult to engage in healthy close relationships. Understanding the distinction between unhealthy intimacy is crucial when navigating these emotional waters. Healthy intimacy involves respect, trust, and open communication, where both individuals feel safe and valued. Unhealthy intimacy, on the other hand, often includes behaviors like excessive dependence or emotional detachment, manipulation, or unresolved conflicts that breed ongoing insecurity and discomfort. By using attachment theory as a guide, you can start recognizing which actions in your relationships foster connections and which ones stem from underlying fears as protective mechanisms.

The influence of attachment on achieving emotional closeness should not be underestimated. It frequently acts as a barrier to the vulnerability of deep bonds since the deeply rooted fear of betrayal or abandonment overshadows the longing for closeness. Overcoming these obstacles typically entails facing and processing these fears in a supportive setting. Therapy can be especially beneficial in this context, as it offers an environment in which to delve into these intricate emotions.

Moreover, forming connections with people who genuinely grasp and honor your need for closeness can gradually reshape your views on intimacy. A practical method for cultivating intimate relationships involves what I refer to as 'progressive exposure.' This process entails increasing your vulnerability levels in a controlled and mindful manner. Begin by making disclosures and sharing thoughts or feelings that may feel slightly uncomfortable but not overwhelming. As you receive reactions from others, your confidence in the safety of intimacy starts to rebuild. Over time, you can expand the scope and depth of your sharing. This approach not only aids in managing the anxiety linked to intimate interactions but also establishes a foundation of trust and empathy in your relationships.

Guide to Progressive Exposure

To assist you in this practice, here's a step-by-step guide to progressive exposure:

1. *Identify Safe People:* Start with individuals who have shown understanding and patience.
2. *Small Disclosures:* Share something personal but not too revealing or vulnerable.
3. *Assess Responses:* Notice and reflect on how these disclosures are received.
4. *Gradual Deepening:* As trust builds, gradually share more deeply or vulnerably.
5. *Reflect and Adjust:* Continuously reflect on your comfort level and the responses you receive, adjusting your approach as needed.

This method isn't about rushing into vulnerability but about gradually increasing your comfort and ability for closeness at a pace that feels natural to you. Each advancement is an affirmation of your capability to participate in intimate relationships, shifting from disorganized attachment patterns to secure and rewarding connections. As you apply these approaches, you might discover that what was once a challenging path transforms into a journey of discovery and bonding.

Communication Skills for Healthier Relationships

Dealing with communication in relationships with a disorganized attachment style can sometimes feel like speaking a foreign language without an interpreter. Your intended messages and emotions can get mixed up, leading to confusion or silence that widens the gap. It's common to send signals or hold back from expressing genuine emotions out of fear of potential consequences. Recognizing these communication challenges is the step towards fostering healthier, more satisfying interactions.

Let's delve into these issues further. Mixed messages often arise when your words convey one thing while your actions or tone suggest another. This can be perplexing for those around you, making it difficult for them to respond appropriately.

Avoiding expressing your feelings may shield you from immediate discomfort or conflicts, but it can also hinder the development of authentic intimacy and understanding in your relationships. These behaviors are often rooted in the underlying complexities of insecure attachments, where the instinct for emotional self-preservation often takes precedence over transparent communication.

Mastering communication techniques is essential to enhancing clarity and effectiveness in communication. Assertiveness empowers you to honestly and directly articulate your thoughts and emotions while still honoring the rights and feelings of others. It all begins with being able to identify your own thoughts and emotions. Before entering into a conversation, take a moment to reflect on your feelings and desired outcomes. This self-awareness will enable you to convey your message effectively.

Active listening is another aspect of effective communication. It involves paying attention to what the speaker is saying rather than just hearing their words passively. Practice maintaining eye contact, nodding in acknowledgment, and refraining from interrupting. After the speaker has spoken, summarize what they said to confirm understanding. This not only deepens engagement but also demonstrates that you value their message.

Validation plays a role in nurturing emotional connections and trust.

Understanding and respecting someone's Emotions, experiences, and thoughts, even if you don't necessarily agree with them, is essential. For instance, acknowledging their perspective by saying, "I understand why you might feel that way" or "It's logical for you to think that" can make a difference in making the other person feel acknowledged and empathized with.

Effective feedback techniques also play a crucial role in improving communication by facilitating mutual understanding and necessary adjustments. When giving feedback, it's important to be specific, focus on the actions rather than the individual, and provide suggestions for improvement. Instead of stating, "You never listen to me," a more constructive approach would be to express how you feel when they are on their phone while you're speaking and suggest keeping devices away during conversations.

Practicing New Communication Skills

To help solidify these communication techniques, consider engaging in role-play exercises. These can be done with a therapist, a trusted friend, or even in a support group. Here's a simple scenario to practice:

Scenario: You feel upset because your friend canceled plans with you at the last minute.

Your Role: Express your feelings using assertive communication, active listening, and validation.

Steps:

1. *Express your feelings clearly*: "I felt disappointed when our plans were canceled at the last minute. I was really looking forward to our time together."
2. *Listen actively*: Allow your friend to explain their reason.

Show you are listening through nods and brief verbal acknowledgments.
3. *Validate their experience:* "I understand that emergencies can come up, and it's not always possible to keep plans."
4. *Use feedback:* "Next time something like this happens, could you send me a quick message earlier? It would help me adjust my plans too."

This activity allows you to practice articulating your needs and handling responses in a setting, boosting your confidence in using these skills in real-world scenarios.

Effective communication goes beyond sharing information; it's about forming transparent, sincere, and respectful connections with others. By refining how you communicate, especially when navigating the complexities of disorganized attachment, you create opportunities for healthier and more fulfilling relationships. Through practice and integration of these strategies into your daily interactions, you may discover that what once seemed challenging evolves into a source of empowerment and closeness.

The Impact of Disorganized Attachment on Romantic Partnerships

The impact of disorganized attachment on romantic relationships can lead to a challenging dance, where partners may unintentionally cause friction due to their uncertainty about navigating the relationship. The push-pull dynamics and sudden breakdowns in communication can be confusing yet familiar, reflecting fears and desires for closeness and independence. Recognizing these patterns is crucial in transforming them into a harmonious connection.

In relationships, the push-pull dynamic often involves alternating between intense closeness and sudden emotional distance. At times, there may be an urge for deep connection driven by a need for security and intimacy. However, when this closeness feels overwhelming, or there is a fear of rejection, partners might withdraw emotionally by putting up barriers. This back-and-forth cycle can leave both individuals feeling confused and hurt, leading to misunderstandings and dissatisfaction.

In a relationship where there's a lack of fear in opening up, conversations can flow smoothly. However, in moments of vulnerability, expressing feelings may become difficult, leading to sudden pauses or unresolved conflicts. Real-life situations shed light on these dynamics and the paths to resolution. Take the case of Elena and Sam... In their late twenties. They were grappling with the aftermath of a shaky disorganized attachment in their relationship. Elena often felt overwhelmed by Sam's desire for closeness, causing her to emotionally retreat abruptly, which left Sam feeling puzzled and rejected. Through couples therapy, they learned to identify these patterns and their origins. By recognizing triggers and communicating openly during tough times, they gradually broke the cycle. They set up a 'safe word' system to indicate when they felt overwhelmed, allowing them to step back and address issues later with a mind.

For partners who don't share the same attachment style, supporting a partner who does can be challenging yet fulfilling. The key is nurturing patience and empathy and making attempts to grasp the fears and needs guiding their partners' actions.

Understanding attachment styles is essential. Recognizing that these behaviors stem from traumas rather than personal rejections can nurture empathy. Having conversations about emotions and needs helps establish trust and mutual understanding in relationships. Partners should regularly reassure each other of their commitment during moments of fear.

Building resilience in relationships involves creating shared experiences that reinforce security and trust. This could include rituals like a weekly 'date night' or daily expressions of appreciation. These practices strengthen the relationship's foundation, making it more resilient to challenges that may trigger behaviors. Engaging in activities like communication workshops or couples therapy can also enhance the bond between partners.

Navigating relationships with a disorganized attachment style is challenging but not impossible. Delving into the underlying dynamics and committing to growth and support, these challenges can lead to deeper connections and understanding between partners. As you both learn to navigate through the tough times, each step forward becomes a journey of mutual progress rather than avoiding missteps.

Strategies for Building Trust with Others

Building trust in relationships can be challenging, especially if past experiences have left you wary due to insecure attachment patterns. Trust within the context of attachment relies on values such as dependability, transparency, and mutual respect. These principles serve as the foundation for relationships, creating a sense of safety that allows for intimacy and emotional openness to thrive. However, when earlier encounters were marked by uncertainty and unpredictability, trusting others may feel daunting. It can seem risky with each step towards trusting someone carrying the weight of betrayal or past hurts.

For individuals grappling with these obstacles, embracing an approach to cultivating trust can be transformative. This strategy involves establishing a series of yet consistent gestures that showcase reliability and predictability in actions. For example, you could begin by sharing personal details with a friend or partner to gauge their sensitivity towards your information. Similarly, agreeing on commitments like regular phone calls can help reinforce trust with each fulfilled promise, gradually rebuilding the foundation of reliability between you and the other person.

Rebuilding trust after experiencing betrayal is a journey that demands a dedicated focus on transparency and consistency. Whether the betrayal stemmed from a broken promise or a significant deception, the road to reconciliation hinges on being candid about one's errors and committing to avoid repeating them. It's crucial to discuss what went wrong, why it happened, and explore strategies to prevent future breaches. This could involve establishing boundaries and expectations that both parties agree upon respecting. Demonstrating consistency in actions, keeping promises, and being present during moments are all essential practices in rebuilding trust. Though it is a process that often requires patience and forgiveness from all involved, it is vital for the healing and strengthening of the relationship.

Integrating exercises aimed at building trust can further enrich this process. Engaging in projects or activities can effectively foster camaraderie and trust. For instance, collaborating on a home improvement task, planning an outing together, or even preparing a meal jointly necessitates coordination, communication, and mutual reliance—all of which nurture trust. Another beneficial exercise involves practicing vulnerability within an environment of openness.

Sharing fears, dreams, and past hurts safely and openly can strengthen trust and deepen bonds in a relationship. Engaging in exercises with a partner or close friend not only builds trust but also enhances the connection on an emotional level, making the relationship stronger and more fulfilling.

Vulnerability Exercise: Sharing Personal Stories

Here's a simple exercise you can try with a partner or close friend to enhance trust through vulnerability:

1. *Set a Comfortable Scene*: Choose a quiet, private setting where you both feel safe and undisturbed.

2. *Agree on Confidentiality:* Ensure that both of you agree whatever is shared will remain confidential.
3. *Take Turns:* One person shares a personal story or feeling that they usually keep private. It should be genuine and meaningful but not overwhelming.
4. *Listen Actively:* The listener should focus entirely on the speaker, showing empathy and withholding judgment.
5. *Reflect and Validate:* After sharing, the listener reflects on what they heard and validates the speaker's feelings without offering solutions or criticism.
6. *Switch Roles:* Reverse roles and repeat the process.

This exercise fosters respect, which is essential for building trust in any relationship. It provides a space for both individuals to be vulnerable, ultimately strengthening their bond of trust with each other.

Establishing trust in the midst of a disorganized attachment can be quite a challenge, but it's also incredibly fulfilling. It opens up opportunities for deeper, more meaningful relationships that offer the support and love everyone craves. As you work on these approaches, always remember that every little effort to build trust is a step towards a stable and connected life.

Co-regulation Techniques for Couples

In the dance of relationships, especially for those dealing with the complexities of disorganized attachment, managing emotional reactions isn't solely dependent on individual abilities. There's strength in co-regulation, a collaborative process where partners assist each other in regulating their emotions. Co-regulation involves creating an atmosphere together that can either calm or stir emotions within each other. Picture two musicians tuning their instruments to blend. Similarly, co-regulation entails adjusting your emotional responses to resonate with one another, fostering feelings of safety and empathy.

One effective technique in co-regulation is synchronized breathing. This straightforward yet impactful practice requires both partners to sit and synchronize their breathing rhythms. It's a demonstration of being 'in sync' with each other and aids in soothing the nervous system, alleviating feelings of tension or unease.

You can try this out by sitting across from each other, closing your eyes, and taking breaths together. This synchronized breathing can be very soothing and act as a physical reminder that you're not going through your emotional journey alone.

Engaging in shared mindfulness activities is also vital to co-regulation. Participating in a mindfulness session, such as guided meditation or a mindful stroll, helps both partners cultivate a sense of peaceful awareness. It allows you to be fully present in the moment, free from past issues or future worries. This joint experience can strengthen your bond and enhance your ability to handle stress as a team. It's about being there for each other, staying connected, and building on the closeness that comes with emotional understanding.

Empathy forms the foundation of co-regulation. It's not just comprehending but also feeling your partner's emotions deeply, which is crucial for responding in ways that meet their emotional needs. Improving responses involves active listening—dedicating yourself entirely to understanding your partner's feelings without rushing to offer solutions or judgments. It means being there for them, acknowledging their emotions, and validating their experiences, even if they differ from yours.

Building a connection with your partner can be really comforting, and often all it takes to make them feel acknowledged and supported. However, co-regulating comes with its set of challenges, and mishaps are not uncommon. These instances might arise from misunderstandings, communication breakdowns, or feeling overwhelmed by our emotions. When things go awry, it's important to see them as opportunities for learning and personal growth. Have discussions about what went south and brainstorm ways to adjust your approach. It could be that one partner needs words of affirmation during tough times, or maybe both need to practice not interrupting when the other is sharing vulnerable feelings. Dealing with these moments honestly and being open to change will improve your co-skills for the future.

Co-regulation Exercise

Try this simple co-regulation exercise to enhance your empathetic connection:

1. *Choose a Quiet Time:* Find a time when both of you are free from distractions and stress.
2. *Share and Reflect:* Take turns sharing something that's currently causing you stress. Limit this to just a few minutes.
3. *Empathize and Validate:* The listening partner should focus solely on understanding and empathizing. Respond with statements that validate feelings, such as "That sounds really tough; I can see why you'd feel that way."
4. *Discuss and Plan:* After both have shared, discuss ways you might help each other manage these stressors in the future.

Engaging in these activities not only helps with managing our emotions moment by moment but also strengthens our understanding and appreciation of each other's feelings. As we navigate the complexities of our relationship, remember that supporting each other is a balance of giving and receiving, a dynamic exchange of tuning into each other's emotional needs and rhythms. By committing to these practices, we strengthen the values of trust and empathy, which are crucial for a solid and loving relationship.

Setting and Respecting Boundaries in Relationships

Setting and honoring boundaries in relationships is crucial for maintaining connections. Boundaries serve as guidelines that define our personal space and interactions with others, playing a vital role in all types of relationships, especially those affected by disorganized attachment styles. It can be challenging to navigate between the fear of being abandoned and the fear of becoming too enmeshed with others, making it essential to establish healthy boundaries.

Boundaries outline what behaviors are acceptable or not within relationships, creating a sense of safety and respect. They are not barriers meant to isolate us but tools that promote positive interactions, ensuring that our needs and the needs of others are acknowledged and met respectfully.

The process of recognizing and setting boundaries begins with understanding your values, desires, and limitations. Start by evaluating which aspects of your relationships bring you joy and which ones cause discomfort or stress. Reflect on experiences to identify any recurring patterns where boundaries may have been crossed or ignored. For example, you might realize that prolonged conversations with a friend who often seeks support without offering it in return leave you feeling emotionally drained. This realization could signal the need to set boundaries regarding the duration of supportive conversations.

Once you've figured out what you need, the next step is to communicate those boundaries effectively. It's important to assert yourself without being aggressive, making sure your voice is heard and respected. Being open and direct about your limits in a way that respects everyone's rights can strengthen relationships. For instance, telling a friend, "I want to support you. I can only chat for 30 minutes today. "sets a clear boundary while showing your commitment to the friendship.

Respecting other's boundaries is just as crucial for building trust and respect in any relationship. It means listening and honoring the limits they set without judgment. If someone asks for time to respect their space instead of pushing for closeness, it demonstrates that you value their autonomy. This mutual respect not only deepens connections but also fosters trust, creating a safe environment where both parties can be open and secure in their interactions.

There may be times when boundaries are crossed, whether intentionally or not. Addressing the breach is essential to upholding the integrity of boundaries and preserving the relationships' well-being.

Start by identifying the breach, then explain how it impacted you, and reiterate your boundaries. If the boundary continues to be ignored, it may be necessary to implement consequences, such as taking a step from the relationship or seeking external support like therapy or mediation. For instance, if a coworker keeps interrupting you in meetings despite your requests to stop, you might have to escalate the matter by talking to a manager or HR for assistance.

Establishing and honoring boundaries is not a one-time event but an ongoing process that requires adaptation and open communication as relationships evolve. By setting boundaries, you not only safeguard your emotional well-being but also establish a foundation for relationships built on mutual respect and understanding. This groundwork allows you to engage with others confidently and comfortably, knowing that your limits are acknowledged and respected. As you navigate your connections with others, remember that each stride toward respected boundaries is a stride toward a healthier, more harmonious life.

Managing Relationship Anxiety

When your heart races and palms sweat at the thought of a conversation with a partner or when your mind spins out of control at the sight of an unanswered text message, you're experiencing what many individuals with disorganized attachment styles encounter as relationship anxiety.

This type of anxiety goes beyond feeling nervous; it involves a deep-seated fear of things going wrong, reflecting past inconsistencies in close relationships that leave behind doubts about one's own value and the trustworthiness of others. The first step to regaining control is understanding what triggers this anxiety. Common triggers include feeling neglected, noticing changes in a partner's behavior or tone, or encountering situations that remind you of past experiences of being abandoned or suffocated. For example, if your partner becomes busy at work and less available, it could trigger anxiety if you associate "busy" with "neglect" based on experiences. Recognizing these triggers is like creating a map of your world; it helps you anticipate and prepare for the emotional challenges that specific actions or situations may bring.

Having a set of relaxation and stress reduction techniques is crucial when dealing with relationship anxiety. Deep breathing is a simple yet effective way to regulate the body's response during moments of high anxiety. This technique involves taking deep breaths to lower heart rate and promote feelings of calmness.

Here's a way you can practice this:

- Breathe in slowly through your nose as you count to four
- Hold your breath for a count of four
- exhale through your mouth for a count of eight

This method not only helps calm your nervous system right away but also shifts your focus from anxious thoughts to your breathing. Progressive muscle relaxation (PMR) is another method, especially when anxiety shows up physically as muscle tension. Begin by tensing each muscle group for five seconds and then relaxing it for 30 seconds, starting from your toes up to your head. This exercise increases awareness of sensations and helps release accumulated stress. Visualization, where you imagine a secure place, can also act as a mental escape from anxiety. Close your eyes. Picture a tranquil setting concentrating on the sensory details—the sounds, sights, and scents. This mental getaway offers a break from relationship stressors, allowing you space to regain emotional balance.

Effective communication skills serve as the connection across the gap of relationship anxiety. Open and sincere communication nurtures. Understanding—key elements that reduce the space for anxiety to thrive.

Begin by practicing expressing your feelings and fears using "I" statements that describe your emotions as your experiences rather than pointing fingers at your partner. For instance, saying, "I feel anxious when we don't discuss our plans," directly conveys how you feel and encourages your partner to understand your emotions without assigning blame. Active listening is also essential; it entails listening and trying to comprehend your partner's viewpoint without immediately formulating a response or defense. This not only validates their feelings but also demonstrates the type of attentive listening you hope to receive in return. These kinds of interactions can significantly reduce misunderstandings. Nurture a stronger emotional bond, creating a more stable foundation that limits anxiety growth.

Lastly, focusing on the moment is crucial for managing relationship anxiety effectively. Mindfulness, which involves being fully present in the moment without judgment, can help you avoid dwelling on past issues or worrying about the future. It enables you to connect with your partner in the here and now, gaining an understanding of where your relationship stands without being clouded by past concerns or future uncertainties. Simple mindfulness practices such as eating or mindful walking, where you concentrate fully on the present experience, can aid in developing this skill.

When you focus on the moment, you're more likely to establish a relationship based on what's happening now rather than dwelling on past worries or future uncertainties. This approach provides both you and your partner with a foundation to grow together. By implementing these techniques in your life, you may notice that the anxiety that once felt overwhelming starts to diminish, giving you the ability to nurture healthy and satisfying relationships. Every effort you make to understand, manage, and express your emotions is a step toward interactions and a more peaceful inner world where relationship anxiety doesn't overshadow your ability to connect with others and experience joy.

Overcoming Impulse Actions in Relationships

When emotions run high like waters, the immediate impulse to react can result in choices that have unintended consequences on your relationships; for individuals with a disorganized attachment, these impulses are often intensified due to past experiences in which heightened emotional responses serve as a necessary defense mechanism. Recognizing this connection is essential; it highlights that your impulsive actions are not weaknesses but coping mechanisms that no longer serve their purpose. They originated from times when uncertainty in relationships demanded defensive reactions. However, these same behaviors can now lead to decisions that put the connections you cherish at risk.

Taming these urges doesn't mean suppressing your feelings. Instead, it's about creating a space between how you feel and what you do, where you can make choices based on reason instead of habit. One helpful strategy is the "24-hour rule," where you give yourself a day to think over decisions or calm down before reacting in the heat of the moment. This pause can prevent you from sending messages that could harm relationships or making choices that you might regret later. Use this time to engage in activities like walking, reading, or hobbies that help relax your mind and emotions. The goal is to delay your response until you have a perspective on the situation and can reply calmly instead of impulsively.

Another helpful method for managing behavior is keeping a thought journal. This simple and impactful practice involves jotting down instances when you feel the urge to act impulsively. Note what triggered the impulse, how it made you feel, what thoughts crossed your mind, and how you reacted. Over time, recurring patterns will emerge—identifying triggers that consistently lead to actions and the thoughts associated with them. This awareness is a step towards making positive changes as it allows you to foresee and plan for situations that might trigger impulsive decisions.

Furthermore, assessing the effectiveness of approaches you've tested will help you refine your methods, enabling you to make choices that align with your relationship goals rather than working against them.

For people dealing with impulsive behaviors, it is a journey that is best not taken alone. Therapy and support groups not only offer guidance but also provide the comfort of knowing that others can relate to your challenges. Working with a professional who specializes in these types of issues can offer personalized techniques for managing impulsiveness based on your individual experiences and requirements. Support groups create a sense of community and the reassurance that you are not facing these struggles by yourself. These environments can serve as havens to delve into your impulses, deeply comprehend their roots, and explore new tactics for handling them. They also offer support and encouragement to help you stay committed to making progress, regardless of how small it may seem.

Embracing the process of controlling behaviors in relationships goes beyond just avoiding missteps; it involves learning how to communicate your emotions and needs in ways that strengthen intimacy rather than diminish it. It's about changing reactions into considerate responses that promote understanding and connection.

As you put these methods into practice, you'll probably notice that your relationships become more stable and fulfilling, reflecting not only who you used to be but also who you're becoming—a person capable of making choices that align with your core values and relationship aspirations. Maneuvering through the complexities of behaviors in relationships can lead to a transformative journey, resulting in not just more consistent interactions but also a deeper self-awareness. As you become more skilled at handling your impulses, you're likely to see your relationships progress into satisfying and supportive bonds. This section has provided you with techniques to identify and control actions enriching your path toward healthier interpersonal connections. As we move on to the next segment, these fundamental skills will become your foundation for more advanced strategies to boost your relationship resilience and emotional intelligence further, ensuring that you aren't just surviving in your relationships but genuinely thriving.

Chapter 4

From Fear to Security: Transitioning Attachment Styles

Imagine standing at the edge of a cliff, with the crashing ocean waves below creating an overwhelming sound. Now, imagine discovering a pathway that leads down to a beach. Each step takes you further from the chaos above and closer to a tranquil shore. This journey from the cliff's edge to the beach symbolizes the transformative process of moving from feeling disorganized and insecure to finding emotional stability and relational harmony.

The Concept of Earned Secure Attachment

The idea of earned attachment offers hope to those who have faced turbulent times due to insecure attachment experiences. It showcases how humans can bounce back and evolve. Earned attachment refers to the psychological shift that occurs when individuals with insecure attachment histories actively work towards developing secure attachment behaviors in adulthood. Unlike those who naturally form disorganized

attachment during childhood, secure individuals who had to earn them have overcome challenges by consciously examining and improving their attachment strategies through reflection, therapy, and personal growth.

Reaching earned security brings emotional benefits on multiple levels. It boosts self-esteem as individuals learn to appreciate themselves and trust in their value.

In terms of relationships, it shows up as increased satisfaction and deeper meaningful bonds with others. Individuals who have developed secure attachments through their experiences can create relationships based on respect and genuine closeness rather than fear and dependence. This shift also helps in building strength, enabling people to face life's challenges with more grace and adaptability, thus reducing the chances of reverting to old harmful behaviors.

The theoretical basis that underpins this journey is solid and has been backed by extensive psychological research over the years. Studies in attachment theory consistently confirm that although early experiences play a role in shaping our attachment styles, these patterns are not fixed. The brain's ability to change and the dynamic nature of our processes mean that change is always possible. Therapeutic approaches focused on repairing attachment have proven effective in assisting individuals in rethinking and reconstructing their views on trust, safety, and connection.

Inspiring Stories of Transformation

Take, for instance, the narrative of "Anna," a woman who grew up in an environment marked by unpredictability and chaos. Her interactions with caregivers who were emotionally distant left her with a fear of being abandoned and an attachment style fraught with disarray that caused turmoil in her adult relationships.

Anna's quest for a sense of security began during therapy, where she delved into the challenges of her past and learned to navigate their impact on her relationships. Through therapy sessions, she started adopting new approaches to self-care and interpersonal connections, gradually moving towards behaviors rooted in trust and stability. Today, Anna not only experiences greater satisfaction in her relationships but also finds a newfound inner peace that was once beyond reach.

Anna's experience is one of many stories that showcase diverse paths and techniques leading to a sense of earned security. These narratives are valuable not only for the hope they inspire but also for the practical insights they provide—strategies that are within reach for anyone willing to embrace a journey of self-transformation. The bravery and dedication demonstrated in these stories serve as a reminder of the potential within each individual to transition from fear to security, from chaos to balance.

As we delve deeper into exploring attachment styles, it's essential to remember these stories. They are more than accounts of personal triumphs; they serve as guides that can assist you on your own quest toward a more secure and meaningful way of interacting with the world.

Every step taken, every plan put into action brings you one step closer to a place of stability and contentment, moving away from the cliffs of fear and uncertainty.

Ways to Foster Healthy Relationship Behaviors

Setting out on the journey toward building secure attachments involves acknowledging and nurturing specific actions that promote stability, trust, and openness in relationships. These actions are the elements of secure attachments and include:

- Consistently responding to relational cues in a supportive manner
- Embracing emotional experiences without overwhelming fear

- Actively seeking and offering support in relationships

Adopting these behaviors may initially seem unfamiliar or challenging for individuals accustomed to the nature of disorganized attachments. However, with effort and dedication to personal development, you can cultivate these healthy relationship behaviors, not only enhancing your connections but also strengthening your feelings of safety and self-value.

One practical method for honing these behaviors is engaging in role-playing exercises. This approach allows you to practice reacting to social scenarios in a controlled and thoughtful way. For instance, you could engage in role-play sessions with a therapist or trusted confidant where you communicate a need or establish boundaries.

The safe environment established during these role plays provides a chance to try out different reactions, receive feedback, and adjust actions in line with the principles of secure attachment. This approach can be beneficial in breaking old habits of disorganized attachment, like withdrawing out of fear or reacting defensively, and instead adopting more positive and supportive ways of engaging.

Keeping a journal is another valuable tool on this journey. By jotting down your daily interactions and emotional responses, you can start recognizing patterns in your behavior that might stem from disorganized attachment. Writing prompts such as "How did I manage challenges today?" and "How did I respond when someone sought my help?" can assist in guiding your reflections. Over time, this habit can boost your self-awareness, enabling you to replace insecure behaviors with secure ones, like offering assistance when needed or openly expressing your feelings.

Integrating mindfulness practices is also essential for developing secure attachment behaviors. Mindfulness promotes a state of attentive awareness of the present moment, aiding in responding more thoughtfully to relational dynamics.

Practicing listening, where you focus entirely on understanding the other person's perspective without jumping to conclusions or being judgmental, can significantly enhance the quality of your interactions. This mindful approach nurtures deeper connections, which are crucial elements of forming strong relationships.

As you add these habits into your daily routine, it's essential to do so gradually and genuinely. Begin by applying these techniques in situations where you feel comfortable and slowly extend them to challenging scenarios. This gradual process helps build self-assurance and resilience, reducing the risk of feeling overwhelmed by the changes you are striving for. Sharing your goals with close friends or family members who can offer support and encouragement is also beneficial. Their understanding and input can be invaluable as you strive to improve your style.

Keeping track of your progress is important for sustaining the momentum of your growth journey. Utilizing tools, like behavior checklists or emotional journals, can assist in monitoring changes over time, offering evidence of your growth. These resources can also pinpoint areas where you may encounter difficulties or require assistance, enabling you to adjust your strategies accordingly. Regularly reviewing your progress with a therapist or a supportive community can provide insights and motivation, strengthening your dedication to fostering secure attachment behaviors.

By engaging in these practices, you're not just aiming for a bond but also laying down a strong emotional foundation that will be there for you in the long run. Each step taken in this journey brings you a step closer to a stable, satisfying, and connected way of living. Remember, change doesn't happen overnight; it takes time, persistence, and kindness towards yourself. Celebrate every win and stay dedicated to your personal growth, knowing that each effort plays a crucial role in your path toward secure attachment.

Role Models and Mentoring in Developing Security

Role models and mentors shape our relationships and emotions. They are like threads woven into the fabric of connections, adding strength and color to our lives. These individuals demonstrate what healthy relationships look like and how to regulate emotions effectively, serving as real-life examples of secure attachment principles in action. Just as children learn language by imitating those around them, adults can also improve their skills by observing and mirroring the behaviors of those who embody secure attachment qualities.

When seeking out role models or mentors, it's essential to find individuals who not only display traits like reliability, empathy, and emotional openness but also resonate with your own values and life experiences.

Role models can come from places, such as a therapist, counselor, or trusted friend. Sometimes, they can also be found in figures or characters from books and movies whose stories inspire resilience and hope. It's essential to look for qualities that align with your growth goals and sense of secure attachment. When choosing a mentor, consider not only their ability to demonstrate secure behaviors but also their willingness to nurture a supportive relationship that fosters your development.

Forming mentoring relationships comes with advantages. Mentors can offer guidance and feedback based on their experiences while addressing your individual challenges. They provide advice and emotional support, reinforcing the lessons learned in therapy or from self-help materials. For instance, a mentor who has achieved secure attachment can offer insights on overcoming intimacy fears or managing relationship anxieties through real-life examples of these principles in action. This bond not only helps establish new behavioral patterns but also provides a safe environment to explore vulnerabilities and acknowledge progress.

Building a Support Network

Establishing a support network is akin to constructing a scaffold around you as you mend and reshape the framework of your style.

This circle of mentors, peers, family members, and friends plays supportive roles. They offer support, practical guidance, and sometimes a reality check to keep you on track with your objectives. Begin by identifying individuals who are emotionally mature and empathetic—those who exhibit secure attachment traits or are actively working on their emotional development.

Initiate conversations to communicate your intention of establishing a growth-focused relationship. Participate in activities that promote bonding and trust, such as gatherings, workshops, or online platforms where experiences and insights can be shared. Over time, this network will become an asset, providing diverse viewpoints and collective wisdom that can help you confront challenges with resilience and embrace growth confidently.

While nurturing these connections, remember that it's as much about giving as it is about receiving. Supporting others in the network not only enhances their lives but also strengthens their own learning journey and personal growth. This fosters a community of assistance and progress towards secure attachment goals. This reciprocal support system forms the groundwork for enduring change, grounding you securely in the practices and principles of secure attachment.

As you delve into the realms of role models, mentors, and supportive networks, reflect on how each bond shapes and mirrors your path toward a sense of self. Every exchange and nugget of guidance internalized adds another layer of strength to the tapestry of your fortitude, reshaping the turmoil of fragmented attachments into a tapestry of peace and steadiness. As you progress, allow these connections to lead and motivate you with each stride marked by education, development, and a closer bond with those in your circle.

Overcoming the Fear of Abandonment

Diving into the psychological depths of abandonment fear, it's critical to understand how this profound anxiety not only roots in your past experiences but also casts shadows over your present interactions and future possibilities. Particularly within the context of disorganized attachment, the fear of abandonment may surface as a formidable barrier, stirring turmoil in relationships and undermining your sense of stability both personally and relationally. This fear often originates from early experiences where primary caregivers were inconsistent or emotionally unavailable, leaving a lasting imprint of insecurity and mistrust. Such early imprints lead to an anticipation of rejection and loss, which perpetuates a cycle of defensive and anxious behaviors in adult relationships.

Addressing and mitigating this pervasive fear involves a multifaceted approach that integrates cognitive-behavioral strategies, principles of exposure therapy, and targeted emotional regulation techniques. Cognitive-behavioral therapy (CBT) offers a structured method to identify and challenge the distorted beliefs and thoughts that fuel your fears. For instance, the belief that "If I get too close to someone, I will inevitably be hurt" can be confronted and reshaped through CBT techniques such as cognitive restructuring, which encourages you to examine the evidence for and against these beliefs and to develop more balanced, realistic thinking patterns.

Exposure therapy principles can also be adapted to help you gradually face situations that trigger your fear of abandonment. This might involve slowly and systematically engaging in behaviors that invoke mild anxiety about abandonment and working your way up to more challenging situations, thereby reducing the fear response through repeated exposures. For example, you might start by sharing minor vulnerabilities with a trusted friend and gradually share more significant aspects of yourself as your comfort level increases. This controlled exposure can help desensitize your emotional responses and build confidence in your ability to handle potential rejection or disappointment.

Emotional regulation strategies are equally crucial in managing the intense emotions that accompany abandonment fear. Techniques such as mindfulness meditation, deep breathing exercises, and progressive muscle relaxation can help soothe your physiological and emotional reactivity, providing a calmer base from which to explore and resolve these fears. These practices not only help in moments of acute stress but also contribute to a longer-term increase in emotional resilience.

Building trust is a vital counterbalance to the fear of abandonment. Developing trust in yourself is foundational, as it strengthens your belief in your ability to cope with challenges and uncertainties in relationships. Self-trust can be nurtured through practices that affirm your capabilities and worth, such as setting and achieving small, personal goals or engaging in self-affirmation exercises. Trust in others can be fostered by choosing to engage in relationships with individuals who consistently demonstrate reliability and empathy. Over time, positive experiences in these relationships can help rewrite old narratives of expectation and fear.

Celebrating both independence and interdependence plays a pivotal role in overcoming abandonment fears. Embracing independence involves recognizing and valuing your own ability to stand alone, make decisions, and take care of yourself, which can significantly boost your confidence and reduce fears of being left alone. On the flip side, celebrating interdependence involves engaging in healthy, supportive relationships where mutual support and connection are valued. Activities that foster interdependence might include collaborative projects, shared hobbies, or support groups where experiences and strengths are exchanged.

Encouraging these practices not only builds a more balanced self-image but also enhances your ability to engage in relationships without overwhelming fear. Each step toward trusting yourself and valuing interdependent connections is a step away from the shadow of abandonment, leading you toward a more secure and fulfilling relational landscape. As you continue to integrate these strategies and celebrate the dual pillars of independence and interdependence, you cultivate a life where fear has less grip and secure, supportive relationships can flourish.

Embracing Vulnerability: Pathway to Secure Attachment

Vulnerability is often misunderstood and seen as a weakness or a path to pain by many. However, viewing vulnerability as a source of strength requires bravery and a shift in perspective, recognizing it as vital for creating intimacy and fostering relationships. True vulnerability involves being open to forming connections and deeper bonds despite the risks of exposure. It entails revealing yourself with all your fears and imperfections and inviting others to understand and embrace you, building mutual trust that is empowering and enriching. Structured and supportive environments are crucial to navigating vulnerability safely, especially if you have faced challenges with patterns in the past. Therapy sessions offer a controlled space where vulnerability can be explored gradually under guidance. Therapists can help you manage your emotions in time by providing feedback and strategies that enhance your comfort level by expressing emotions openly.

Support groups create a sense of community where you and other people can share their vulnerabilities and feel understood and supported by others who can relate to their experiences. These groups help normalize feelings of vulnerability and create an environment of safety and acceptance for people to express their selves.

Embracing vulnerability goes beyond therapy or support groups as it allows for connections with others, leading to more genuine and fulfilling relationships. Sharing emotions openly enriches interactions, enabling others to connect with your self and build stronger relational bonds. It also enhances self-awareness and emotional intelligence by helping you recognize and communicate your feelings effectively.

While being vulnerable can have its challenges, such as facing rejection or disappointment, it is essential to view these experiences as opportunities for growth rather than failures. Each setback offers lessons about your boundaries, needs, and the importance of trust in relationships. Dealing with challenges like these requires having a support system of friends and family who can offer comfort and perspective. It's also important to practice self-care activities such as mindfulness and self-compassion to bounce back from situations and strengthen your ability to face vulnerability without being consumed by fear.

Handling Setbacks

To better handle setbacks that may come with being vulnerable, try keeping a resilience journal. Write down moments when vulnerability led to both negative outcomes. Reflect on the lessons learned from each experience, consider how you could approach things differently in the future, and think about ways to support yourself during healing. This habit not only boosts your resilience but also reminds you of your progress and inner strength gained from each experience, motivating you to embrace vulnerability as an essential part of your journey toward building secure connections.

As you progress, remember that every step toward vulnerability is a step toward a fulfilling, interconnected life. It's a process that nurtures closeness and trust, reshaping how you interact with others and yourself. Embrace each instance of openness, with bravery and patience, understanding that the road to secure relationships is paved with vulnerability, authenticity, and resilience.

Reparenting Yourself Towards Security

"Embracing the idea of reparenting oneself may seem unfamiliar at first. It's deeply rooted in psychological growth practices. It involves adopting nurturing and supportive behaviors towards oneself for those who lacked consistent care or empathy in their early years. Reparenting allows you to offer yourself the love and care you may have missed out on, aiding in healing wounds and developing healthier relationships with yourself and others.

This process includes steps to address your emotional and psychological needs. The initial step is acknowledging the needs of your child and recognizing moments of vulnerability or distress that reflect unmet childhood needs. Listening to these emotions can reveal what your inner child requires for healing. The next step involves showing self-compassion by treating your pain with kindness and understanding as you would for a loved one or a child."It also means challenging any negative or self-doubting thoughts with positive affirmations of self-worth and self-acceptance. Establishing boundaries is another crucial aspect of reparenting. For individuals with disorganized attachment styles, boundaries may have been too rigid or too loose in the past. Learning to set appropriate boundaries with others is a way of caring for your inner child by not allowing others to mistreat you or drain your energy without your consent. This could involve saying no to responsibilities when you're already feeling overwhelmed or choosing to distance yourself from relationships that feel more draining than nurturing.

Therapy facilitates the process of reparenting. A therapist can create an environment for you to explore past wounds without judgment, guide you in understanding how your childhood experiences influenced your current attachment style, and help you develop healthier ways of relating to yourself. For example, they may lead you through exercises that enable communication, with your child offering comfort and reassurance to neglected or wounded parts of yourself from the past.

The lasting advantages of reparenting are profound. By addressing and healing your child's wounds, you can significantly diminish disorganized attachment behaviors over time.

This process of healing encourages growth and results in the development of a secure attachment style, which is characterized by increased emotional stability and healthier relationships. Individuals who have effectively nurtured themselves often express a sense of wholeness and integration, having addressed core elements of their self-perception that were previously fragmented or distressing.

Self-nurturing is not a solution but a gradual, ongoing journey of providing oneself with the care and love that may have been lacking but always deserved. By learning to nurture oneself, one gradually transforms one's self-relationship and, consequently, their relationships with others. Every act of kindness towards your child paves the way for a more confident, secure, and harmonious self. These changes extend into all aspects of life, enriching interactions and enabling engagement with others from a place of resilience and genuineness. Remember that each small step on this path contributes to a transformative journey—one that leads to a more fulfilled and emotionally resilient version of yourself.

Using Positive Psychology to Reinforce security

Using the principles of psychology to strengthen security is a notable approach in the realm of mental well-being and personal development. Unlike methods that focus on fixing weaknesses, positive psychology emphasizes the importance of nurturing virtues and strengths to enhance one's quality of life. This field is based on the idea that individuals strive for a satisfying existence, emphasizing promoting happiness and overall well-being as vital elements in forming secure connections. By shifting the perspective from problems to growth, positive psychology offers a refreshing outlook on how one can progress toward emotional stability and more fulfilling relationships.

A core aspect of psychology lies in fostering positive emotions such as gratitude, joy, hope, and contentment – emotions that go beyond momentary feelings. These emotions serve as anchors that help maintain balance and cultivate a lasting sense of security. Gratitude, for example, involves acknowledging and valuing the positives in one's life, which can significantly alter one's outlook from scarcity or fear to abundance and gratitude. Regularly appreciating the people, experiences, or simple joys that bring happiness can strengthen pathways associated with positivity and counteract negative tendencies often found in insecure attachment styles.

Joy is another emotion that rejuvenates the spirit and boosts resilience. Engaging in activities that bring you joy or connecting with uplifting people can nurture positivity. Hope is essential for facing life's uncertainties, and optimism makes challenges seem surmountable and goals more attainable. These emotions aren't just passive; they can be actively promoted through habits aligned with psychology.

Developing resilience, an aspect of positive psychology, is crucial for those transitioning from insecure to secure attachment styles. Resilience will let you bounce back from setbacks and continue growing despite obstacles. It involves maintaining a mindset, honing skills, and adopting behaviors that help cope effectively with life's challenges. Resilience is akin to a muscle—it grows stronger through practice and use. Engaging in resilience-building activities like problem-solving, staying hopeful, and seeking support can improve your ability to navigate relationship dynamics.

Positive Psychology Interventions

To incorporate psychology into your daily routine, you may want to try specific interventions known to boost spirits and emotional well-being. One way to practice gratitude is to keep a gratitude journal where you write down three things you're thankful for each day.

Engaging in these activities not only helps you shift your focus away from what is lacking or troubling in your life but also fosters a sense of well-being and connection. Acts of kindness are another practice that involves small, thoughtful gestures done without expecting anything in return. Whether it's lending a hand to a neighbor, volunteering your time, or simply offering a word to someone you don't know, these actions can significantly lift your spirits and positively impact those around you, creating waves of positivity. Furthermore, embracing optimism means choosing to see the potential for positive outcomes instead of dwelling on worst-case scenarios. Techniques like envisioning the possible outcomes across different aspects of your life can strengthen your pathways to hope and anticipation of favorable results.

By integrating these practices into your routine, you not only enhance your personal well-being but also cultivate stronger and more fulfilling relationships. Positive psychology provides transformative tools aimed at reshaping not only how you feel but also the overall quality of your life. As you continue to incorporate these principles into your life, you may notice that the world appears a bit brighter, and challenges become more manageable. Relationships are enriched with shared joy and gratitude.

Every positive step you take brings you closer to a life filled with depth and stronger connections, reflecting the core values of positive psychology.

Breaking the Cycle of Seeking validation

Breaking free from the cycle of seeking validation is crucial in navigating life's dance, where we each move to the beat of our needs and desires. The pursuit of validation can often lead us astray, especially when it originates from feelings of insecurity and disorganized attachment. Recognizing this quest and reshaping it into a journey toward self-validation can be both empowering and challenging.

Seeking validation often manifests as a chase for approval from others, mirroring our own doubts about self-worth. It may involve sacrificing your needs to accommodate others or adjusting your beliefs to fit in with those around you in the hope of feeling accepted and loved. These behaviors stem from a voice that questions your value and worthiness of love and respect.

This constant quest for validation is typically triggered by inconsistent affirmations received during early developmental stages, leaving behind lingering doubts about self-perception.

To break free from this pattern, it's essential to start by embracing a mindset that values validation. This involves boosting your self-esteem from within and cultivating a sense of independence that remains steady even when faced with external uncertainties.

Fostering validation includes practicing self-compassion and self-acceptance. Simple activities like self-talk can make a big difference. By replacing self-dialogue with affirmations that recognize your worth and abilities, such as "I am worthy," "I deserve love and respect," and "My feelings matter, " you can rewire your subconscious to embrace your inherent value.

It's also crucial to set expectations in relationships to reduce the need for external validation. Understanding that while relationships can bring joy, they shouldn't be the basis of your self-worth is key. Relying on others to validate your emotions or choices can lead to disappointment and reinforce dependency. Instead, focus on fostering connections that are mutually supportive and promote growth and respect. In relationships, validation becomes a two-way street rather than a one-sided need.

Achieving goals can boost self-esteem and reduce the need for validation from others. By setting and reaching milestones in areas like work, hobbies, or self-improvement, you prove your capabilities and value without relying on approval. Each accomplishment, big or small, enhances your confidence and validates your skills, lessening the urge to seek validation externally.

As you adopt these habits, you'll see a change in how you view and engage with the world. Freed from seeking others' opinions and acceptance, you'll have the liberty to be yourself authentically and form connections based on mutual admiration and respect. This newfound independence doesn't mean isolation; instead, it allows for relationships built on security and self-assurance, knowing that your worth isn't tied to someone's Recognition.

Welcome this transformation with patience and kindness toward yourself as old patterns are shed over time. Every step forward brings you closer to a genuine existence where your value is acknowledged and celebrated primarily by yourself.

Reflect on the impact of looking within for validation as we wrap up our discussion on breaking the cycle of seeking external approval. This process not only influences how you interact with others but also enhances your own self-esteem, creating a stronger and more lasting sense of self-worth. As you progress, take along the knowledge and perspectives acquired and venture into the phase of personal development with assurance and a clear vision prepared to delve into fresh aspects of emotional and social balance.

Chapter 5

Healing from Past Traumas

Picture yourself standing at the crossroads of your past and present, where every path you take echoes with footsteps both old and new. These are the trails marked by your experiences, and among them are those shadowed by trauma. For many, understanding the intricate dance between past traumas and present behaviors isn't just academic—it's a deeply personal quest for peace and stability. In this chapter, we embark on a compassionate exploration of how traumas, particularly those rooted in early childhood, intertwine with our attachment styles, influencing the very fabric of our relationships and self-perception. Here, we also affirm the transformative power of addressing and healing these wounds, not just to mend but to thrive.

The Connection Between Trauma and Attachment Styles

Trauma, especially in the tender years of childhood, can profoundly influence the development of attachment styles. When a child experiences trauma, the response of their caregivers to their distress plays a crucial role in shaping their future interactions. If a caregiver provides consistent comfort and protection, the child learns to associate relationships with safety and reliability. However, if the caregiver is a source of fear or fails to soothe the child's distress adequately, this can lead to the development of a disorganized attachment style. In such cases, relationships might be perceived as both necessary for survival and inherently dangerous, creating a confusing internal conflict that can last into adulthood.

The impact of trauma extends beyond immediate emotional responses; it can cause enduring changes to brain regions involved in attachment and emotional regulation. Neuroscientific research reveals that trauma can alter the amygdala, hippocampus, and prefrontal cortex—areas critical for processing emotions and managing stress. For instance, an overactive amygdala can heighten fear responses, making it difficult to feel safe even in non-threatening situations. Similarly, if the hippocampus is affected, it might impair the ability to form coherent memories or make it challenging to distinguish between past trauma and present circumstances. These changes can make emotional regulation a formidable task, often leading those with disorganized attachment into a perpetual state of hyperarousal or emotional shutdown.

The long-term effects of unresolved trauma are manifold, penetrating deep into the realms of relationships, self-image, and overall emotional well-being. Individuals may find themselves in a cycle of unstable relationships, perpetually seeking safety but subconsciously sabotaging connections that feel too close or too real. This pattern not only strains relationships but can also erode self-esteem, as the individuals may blame themselves for their relational failures. Moreover, unresolved trauma can manifest as various psychological issues, including anxiety, depression, and PTSD, which further complicate personal development and the ability to form secure attachments.

Addressing these traumas is not merely beneficial; it is essential for anyone seeking to resolve attachment issues and build healthier, more stable relationships. Healing from trauma involves more than just understanding its impact—it requires active engagement in therapeutic practices that can help reprocess and integrate traumatic memories. This healing is foundational, as it not only helps individuals develop healthier attachment patterns but also significantly improves their quality of life. Therapy, mindfulness practices, and supportive relationships play pivotal roles in this process, offering paths to recover and rediscover a sense of safety and trust in connections with others.

Reflection Section

Consider this: Reflect on moments in your past that seem to echo in your present interactions. How do you feel these experiences have shaped your view of safety and trust in your relationships? Acknowledging these influences can be your first step toward healing and reshaping your attachment style.

As we continue to explore the depths of trauma and its impact on our lives, remember that the journey to healing is not just about revisiting past pains but about unlocking the doors to a more secure and fulfilling future. Each step you take towards understanding and uncovering your traumas paves the way for more authentic and stable relationships—both with yourself and with others.

Therapeutic Approaches to Healing Attachment Wounds

When you consider the journey to mend the deep-seated wounds of disorganized attachment, therapy stands as a beacon of hope and transformation. Various therapeutic approaches have been tailored to address the complexities of attachment wounds, and among them, psychodynamic therapy, cognitive-behavioral therapy (CBT), and attachment-based therapy are particularly noteworthy. Each of these therapies offers unique perspectives and tools that cater to the intricate layers of trauma and its aftermath on attachment styles.

Psychodynamic therapy delves into the unconscious patterns of your behavior, which are often rooted in early childhood experiences. It helps you uncover and understand the unconscious dynamics that influence your current relationships and emotional reactions. This form of therapy is particularly beneficial for those who might not even be aware of how past trauma is influencing their present, as it brings these subconscious patterns to light in a supportive and safe environment. Cognitive-behavioral therapy (CBT), on the other hand, provides a more structured approach, focusing on identifying and changing negative thought patterns and behaviors. In the context of disorganized attachment, CBT can be incredibly effective in helping you develop healthier ways of thinking and reacting to emotional triggers, thereby reducing the chaos that often infiltrates your relationships and self-perception.

Attachment-based therapy specifically targets issues surrounding attachment styles. It is designed to rebuild or create a secure attachment style, offering you a corrective emotional experience through the therapeutic relationship itself. This type of therapy emphasizes the importance of developing a safe, trusting relationship with the therapist, who acts as a stand-in for the consistent, supportive caregiver you might have missed during your formative years. This relationship can provide a new, healthier template for emotional connections, teaching you that relationships can be safe, reliable, and nurturing.

The role of the therapeutic relationship in these treatments cannot be overstated. For individuals grappling with disorganized attachment, the therapeutic relationship offers a vital corrective emotional experience. It creates a safe space where you can explore vulnerabilities without fear of judgment or rejection—a stark contrast to previous experiences that may have taught you to expect hurt or betrayal from close relationships. This trusting relationship with a therapist can become a model for future relationships, challenging old patterns and encouraging new, healthier ways of connecting with others.

Case Examples

Consider the case of "Elena," a client who came into therapy struggling with intense fears of abandonment and a pattern of sabotaging her relationships. Through psychodynamic therapy, Elena uncovered that these fears stemmed from early experiences with a caregiver who was emotionally unavailable and unpredictably punitive. Understanding these patterns was a revelation for Elena, allowing her to see how they had colored her expectations of all close relationships. Through ongoing work, focusing on building a trusting relationship with her therapist, Elena gradually began to feel safer in her relationships outside of therapy, learning to trust and open herself to the possibility of true intimacy and connection.

Another case is "Tom," who engaged in CBT to address his disorganized attachment manifesting in erratic behaviors within his marriage. Tom learned to identify his automatic negative thoughts and the behaviors they triggered, such as withdrawal or aggression. Through CBT techniques, he developed new, healthier thought patterns and learned practical skills for communicating his needs and emotions more effectively. This not only improved his relationship with his spouse but also significantly reduced his overall anxiety and self-doubt, demonstrating the profound impact of tailored therapeutic approaches on healing attachment wounds.

Choosing the right therapy involves a careful consideration of your specific needs, circumstances, and comfort level. When selecting a therapeutic approach, it's crucial to consider what resonates most with you. Are you looking for a therapy that digs deep into the roots of your emotional struggles, or do you prefer a more structured approach that offers clear strategies and goals? It might also be beneficial to consult with a few therapists before making a decision. Many therapists offer initial consultations, which can give you a sense of their approach and whether the dynamic feels supportive and comfortable for you.

As you navigate the options available, remember that the goal is to find a therapeutic experience that feels like a good fit—one that respects your pace, acknowledges your experiences, and supports your growth toward a more secure and fulfilling life. This exploration into therapeutic approaches is not just about healing past wounds; it's about empowering you to forge deeper, more meaningful connections and reclaiming a life defined not by trauma but by resilience and hope.

Integrating Body-Based Therapies for Trauma Release

When you consider the profound impact trauma can have on both the mind and body, it becomes clear that healing must also address the physical as well as the psychological. Body-based therapies like somatic experiencing, trauma-sensitive yoga, and body psychotherapy provide a crucial avenue for this kind of holistic healing. These therapies are grounded in the understanding that trauma is not just remembered by the mind but also held in the body—in the tightening of muscles, the quickening of breath, and the tensing of the shoulders. By focusing directly on the body, these therapies help release the physical manifestations of trauma, facilitating a deeper, more integrated healing process.

Somatic experiencing, developed by Dr. Peter Levine, is particularly effective in addressing the physical symptoms of trauma. This therapeutic approach is based on the study that animals in the wild, despite regular threats to their lives, do not exhibit symptoms of trauma. Levine concluded that this is because they utilize innate mechanisms to regulate and discharge the energy associated with survival behaviors. Somatic experiencing helps you tap into these natural coping mechanisms by guiding you through physical sensations associated with traumatic memories. The therapy gently encourages the release of pent-up trauma-related energy through physical movements or exercises that promote healing, grounding, and comfort.

Trauma-sensitive yoga, another key body-based therapy, incorporates traditional yoga practices but adapts them to be mindful of the needs of individuals who have experienced trauma. This adaptation involves creating a safe, predictable space where you can learn to reconnect with your body at your own pace. The yoga poses and breathing exercises are designed to help build attunement to the body, which can often feel like an enemy post-trauma. By focusing on the present moment and bodily sensations in a non-judgmental space, trauma-sensitive yoga helps to restore a sense of control and ownership over your body, which is often compromised in trauma.

Body psychotherapy integrates psychotherapeutic and bodywork techniques to address the psychological and somatic symptoms of trauma. It operates on the premise that the mind and body are interconnected and that psychological distress can manifest as physical symptoms. Through techniques such as deep tissue massage, movement patterns, and breathing exercises, body psychotherapy aims to release the physical tension that is symptomatic of emotional distress. This release not only alleviates physical discomfort but also significantly impacts emotional and psychological well-being.

Practical Exercises: Guided Grounding Technique

To begin addressing the physical manifestations of trauma, try this simple grounding exercise:

1. Find a comfortable and quiet spot to sit or lie down without interruption.
2. Close your eyes and take a few deep, slow breaths to center yourself.
3. Focus your attention on your feet. Notice any sensations as you consciously relax your feet. Imagine tree roots growing

from the bottom of your feet. Slowly, these roots are reaching deep into the earth, anchoring you securely.
4. Gradually move your attention up your body, part by part—legs, abdomen, chest, arms, neck, and head. At each stage, pause and allow yourself to relax and release any tension you notice.
5. With each breath, imagine warmth and relaxation spreading across each part of your body.
6. Once you've moved through your entire body, sit quietly for a few moments, enjoying the sensation of being grounded and present in your body.

The benefits of releasing bodily trauma through these therapies are profound and far-reaching, especially in the context of disorganized attachment. As physical tensions related to past traumas are released, you may find a corresponding easing of emotional tensions. This can lead to improved emotional regulation, as the body no longer perpetuates a state of heightened alertness that disrupts emotional balance. Additionally, as your body becomes a safer, more comfortable place, your capacity for forming secure attachments can improve. Feeling secure within yourself enhances your ability to nurture healthy, stable relationships with others, which is often compromised in those with disorganized attachment.

Supporting these claims, research and case studies from the field of somatic psychology underscore the effectiveness of body-based therapies in treating trauma. Studies have shown that interventions focusing on bodily engagement and awareness can significantly reduce symptoms of PTSD, anxiety, and depression, all of which are common in individuals with histories of trauma and disorganized attachment. These findings highlight the essential role that bodily therapies play in addressing not just the mental but also the physical echoes of trauma, paving the way for a more integrated and whole form of healing.

The Role of EMDR in Resolving Attachment Issues

Eye Movement Desensitization and Reprocessing (EMDR) is a form of psychotherapy that has been gaining recognition for its effectiveness in processing and alleviating the distress associated with traumatic memories. Developed by Francine Shapiro in the late 1980s, EMDR is based on the premise that our minds can heal from psychological trauma much as our bodies recover from physical trauma. When you cut your finger, your body works naturally to heal the wound. If an unknown object or repeated injury irritates the wound, it festers and causes pain. Once the block is removed, the healing process can resume. EMDR asserts that a similar sequence of events occurs with our mental processes. Tbrain's information processing system naturally moves toward mental health unless it is blocked by the impact of a disturbing event. EMDR therapy shows that a similar sequence of events occurs with mental processes. Tbrain's information processing system naturally moves toward mental health. If the system is blocked or imbalanced by the weight of a disturbing event, the emotional wound festers and can cause intense suffering.

Using EMDR, therapists help clients activate their natural healing processes through a structured protocol that includes the client focusing simultaneously on spontaneous associations of traumatic images, thoughts, emotions, and bodily sensations and bilateral stimulation, most commonly through repeated eye movements.

For individuals grappling with disorganized attachment—a style often rooted in unresolved trauma—EMDR offers a particularly potent therapeutic option. This therapy is especially adept at helping individuals reprocess distressing memories that are the groundwork for their attachment issues. By desensitizing the emotional impact of these memories, EMDR aids in transforming the chaotic narratives into organized, integrated memories. This reprocessing is crucial for individuals who have experienced inconsistent caregiving, as it allows them to form a coherent narrative of their past experiences, reducing the disorganization in their thoughts and, consequently, their relationships.

An EMDR session typically follows a structured eight-phase approach, starting with history-taking and ending with evaluation. In one of the key middle phases, the client focuses on a traumatic memory while simultaneously engaging in bilateral stimulation, such as side-to-side eye movements. This dual attention task is believed to facilitate the biological mechanisms involved in Rapid Eye Movement (REM) sleep, which helps in processing unconscious material. It's essential to note that EMDR is not simply about eye movements—it integrates elements of cognitive therapy with imaginal exposure used in a structured protocol informed by the Adaptive Information Processing model. This approach ensures that the emotional distress is fully processed, leading to a significant decrease or elimination of trauma-induced symptoms and behaviors.

For those considering this therapeutic path, understanding what to expect during an EMDR session can significantly ease any apprehensions. Initially, you and your therapist will spend time mapping out specific traumatic memories and identifying current situations that cause emotional distress. Subsequent sessions will focus on processing these memories through guided eye movements, all while the therapist aids in navigating the emotional landscape that arises. It's a journey through past pains that leads to a significant reduction in the emotional weight these memories hold, promoting a healthier integration of past experiences.

Supporting the efficacy of EMDR, numerous research studies have underscored its benefits in treating trauma-related issues across various populations. For instance, randomized controlled trials have consistently shown that EMDR therapy effectively decreases the symptoms of post-traumatic stress disorder (PTSD), with some studies showing that it is more rapid in achieving effects than other forms of therapy. Furthermore, research also highlights EMDR's ability to improve aspects of emotional regulation—a crucial element for those dealing with disorganized attachment, as better regulation can lead to more secure and organized attachment behaviors.

As you consider the potential paths for healing and transformation, EMDR presents a unique and scientifically backed option that addresses the roots of disorganized attachment by processing the traumatic memories that often underpin it. It's a therapy that not only aims to heal but to empower, giving you the tools to reclaim your narrative and, ultimately, your relationships.

Creating a Personalized Healing Ritual

In the intricate tapestry of healing, personalized rituals act as threads that not only mend but also strengthen and beautify the overall design. These rituals, crafted from your unique experiences and tailored to your specific emotional landscape, offer a profound sense of control and empowerment—essential elements in the healing journey from trauma. The importance of these rituals lies in their ability to anchor you, providing a consistent practice that can bring comfort and predictability in times of emotional turbulence. They create a sacred space and time where healing can flourish, untouched by the external chaos that often accompanies day-to-day life.

Creating your healing ritual begins with a deep understanding of your needs and the specific areas where you seek healing. This might involve sitting quietly with yourself, perhaps in a meditative state, to really listen to what your heart and body are telling you. What brings you peace? What activities help you feel grounded and connected to yourself? For some, this might be a daily walk in nature, feeling the earth underfoot and the rhythm of their breath aligning with the steps they take. For others, it could involve morning pages—a journaling technique where you write a stream of consciousness thoughts every morning to clear your mind and connect with your inner voice.

Once you have identified what resonates with you, the next step is to structure these activities into a ritual. This means setting aside a specific time and place each day (or week, depending on your routine) to engage in this practice. Consistency is key here; it's what transforms a simple activity into a ritual. This regular commitment to your healing practice acts as a powerful affirmation to yourself that you are worth the time and effort, reinforcing your sense of self-worth and aiding in emotional recovery.

Let's explore some examples of healing rituals that have helped others on similar paths. Daily affirmations can be potent in shifting negative thought patterns. You might start each day by stating affirmations that foster self-compassion and acceptance, such as "I am worthy of love and healing" or "I release my past and forgive myself." Over time, these affirmations can help reshape your internal narrative, which is often critical in individuals recovering from trauma.

Another effective ritual involves dedicating quiet time for mindfulness or meditation. This practice can significantly enhance your awareness of the present moment, helping to alleviate the grip of past traumas that often cloud your emotional world. By focusing on your breath, or perhaps on a guided visualization, you allow yourself a reprieve from the constant chatter of the mind, which is incredibly healing for those with disorganized attachment styles, as it fosters a sense of internal safety and calm.

It is also vital to allow your rituals the flexibility to evolve as you do. What serves you at the beginning of your healing process may need adjustment as you grow and your needs change. This adaptation is not a sign of failure but rather an indication of your deepening self-awareness and changing emotional landscape. Regularly revisiting and tweaking your rituals ensures that they remain relevant and supportive, genuinely reflecting your journey and supporting your growth at every stage.

Embracing these personalized healing rituals is about more than just managing symptoms or temporary relief—it's about crafting a lifestyle that supports sustained healing and personal empowerment. These rituals remind you regularly of your resilience and capacity to heal, reinforcing a positive self-image and fostering a nurturing internal environment conducive to growth. As you integrate these practices into your life, observe how they influence not just your moments of practice but also the broader spectrum of your daily existence. The peace, stability, and joy you cultivate during your rituals can begin to infuse your overall life, transforming not just moments but entire days and beyond.

Support Systems and Their Role in Healing Trauma

In the healing landscape, a robust support system acts not just as a scaffolding but as an essential foundation that offers stability, comfort, and practical aid. For those navigating the aftermath of trauma, the presence of a supportive network can be transformative, significantly enhancing the healing journey. It's akin to having a team where each member brings their own set of tools and strengths, contributing to a more comprehensive and effective recovery process. Emotional support from loved ones can help create a buffer against the isolating effects of trauma. At the same time, practical assistance can help manage the day-to-day challenges that might otherwise overwhelm your capacity to cope.

Building or strengthening your support network is pivotal, and it begins with identifying the individuals in your life who provide empathy, understanding, and non-judgmental support. These might be friends, family members, colleagues, or even mental health professionals. The key is to cultivate these relationships actively, ensuring they are built on trust and mutual respect. Additionally, participating in support groups can be beneficial. These groups provide a space to share experiences and strategies with others who have dealt with the same challenges as you, creating a sense of community and shared understanding that is profoundly reassuring.

Utilizing community resources is another strategic layer in building your support network. Many communities offer services such as counseling, support groups, educational workshops, and more. Engaging with these resources not only broadens your support network but also connects you with professional guidance and peer support, which can be crucial during times of intense emotional need. The act of reaching out and connecting with these resources can in itself be empowering, reaffirming your agency in your healing process.

Navigating relationships during this time is equally crucial. Trauma can strain personal relationships, especially if those around you are unfamiliar with the ways trauma can affect behavior and emotions. Communicating your needs clearly and setting healthy boundaries are essential strategies in maintaining and nurturing relationships during your healing journey. Boundaries help define what you are comfortable with and how others can support you without overstepping, ensuring interactions remain respectful and supportive. Moreover, effective communication helps those around you understand your experiences and needs better, enabling them to support you in ways that are truly beneficial rather than inadvertently triggering.

The impact of peer support, particularly from those who have experienced similar traumas, can be uniquely powerful. Sharing your story with peers can validate your experiences and emotions, reducing feelings of isolation and alienation. This shared empathy not only fosters deeper connections but also promotes mutual healing. The act of supporting others can also reinforce your own coping strategies and insights, further enhancing your resilience and recovery. Peer support groups often provide a collective strength that can be incredibly empowering, offering hope and shared paths to recovery that might seem daunting to walk alone.

As you lean into the support of your community and loved ones, remember that each interaction, each shared story, and each offered hand is a step towards not just healing but also rediscovering the strength and connection that trauma often obscures. This network of support is not a luxury—it is a vital component of your healing journey, providing the emotional and practical backing necessary to navigate the challenges of recovery from trauma. As you continue to weave these threads of support into your life, they become integral to your healing, transforming the tapestry of your experiences into one marked by resilience, connection, and renewal.

As we reflect on the profound role of support systems in healing from trauma, we recognize that recovery is not a solitary endeavor but a communal journey enriched by each connection and supported interaction. The next chapter will venture deeper into the specific healing therapies and interventions that can further facilitate this journey, providing you with additional tools and strategies to support your path to recovery. This exploration will not only expand your understanding of the therapeutic options available but also empower you with the knowledge to choose the best strategies for your unique circumstances.

Chapter 6

Practical Tools for Everyday Challenges

Interacting in the social world with a disorganized attachment style can sometimes feel like trying to decipher a complex dance without knowing the steps. You might experience moments of synchrony, feeling connected and in tune with those around you, only to suddenly find yourself stepping on toes or falling out of rhythm. This chapter is dedicated to equipping you with practical strategies designed to enhance your social skills, manage social anxiety, build resilience, and create meaningful connections—turning those awkward missteps into a graceful dance.

Navigating Social Interactions with Confidence

Social interactions are fundamental to our well-being, offering avenues for support, joy, and shared experiences. Yet, for those grappling with disorganized attachment, these interactions can be sources of significant stress and anxiety. Enhancing your social skills is akin to learning a new language—a language of gestures, expressions, and words that, when understood, can transform your social experiences from confusing or stressful to enriching and enjoyable.

One of the cornerstone skills in this social toolkit is active listening. Active listening involves fully focusing on what is being said rather than just passively hearing the speaker's words. It means listening with all senses—paying attention not only to the story but also to the emotions behind the words. Practicing active listening can significantly improve your interactions. It makes the speaker feel valued and shows that you are genuinely engaged. You can practice this skill in everyday conversations by focusing entirely on the other person, avoiding distractions, and reflecting back on what you've heard to confirm your understanding. This practice not only deepens your relationships but also enhances your ability to perceive and respond to the underlying feelings in social exchanges.

Maintaining eye contact is another vital social skill. It signals confidence and interest in the conversation. However, for someone with a disorganized attachment style, sustaining eye contact might feel particularly challenging, potentially triggering feelings of vulnerability or fear. If this resonates with you, start small. Practice by maintaining eye contact for a few seconds at a time during conversations, gradually increasing the duration as you become more comfortable. This gradual exposure can help ease your anxiety over time, making social interactions feel more natural and connected.

Engaging in small talk, though often underrated, is a powerful tool to open doors to deeper conversations. It acts as a bridge, allowing you to connect with others over common ground. If small talk feels daunting, prepare a few go-to topics in advance—like commenting on the environment, asking about recent movies or books, or discussing a shared interest. These prepared topics can ease the pressure of finding something to say, helping you navigate social settings more confidently.

Role-Playing Exercises

Consider engaging in role-playing exercises with a friend or therapist to practice these skills in a safe environment. For instance, simulate a social event where you practice active listening, maintain eye contact, and initiate small talk. This safe practice can boost your confidence and prepare you for real-life social interactions.

Managing social anxiety is another critical aspect of navigating social settings. Techniques like deep breathing exercises can be incredibly effective in managing physiological symptoms of anxiety. When you feel your anxiety escalating, try taking slow, deep breaths—inhale for a count of four, hold for a count of four, and exhale for a count of four. This breathing pattern can help calm your nervous system and reduce the immediate symptoms of anxiety, allowing you to engage more fully in social interactions.

Positive self-talk is another powerful tool. Before entering a social situation, encourage yourself with affirmations such as "I am capable of handling social interactions" or "I am worthy of making connections." This positive reinforcement can boost your self-esteem and reduce feelings of anxiety.

To build resilience in social settings, develop the habit of reflecting on and learning from each social interaction. Whether an interaction goes well or presents challenges, take some time afterward to think about what happened, what went well, what could be improved, and how you can apply these learnings to future interactions. This reflection not only builds your social skills but also enhances your resilience, helping you recover more quickly from social setbacks or rejections.

Creating meaningful connections in social settings is about showing genuine interest in others and sharing your experiences in a balanced way. People naturally gravitate towards those who seem interested in their lives. Ask open-ended questions to encourage others to talk about themselves and listen actively to what they share. Reciprocate by sharing your own experiences and feelings, which can nurture a deeper connection and mutual understanding.

As you continue to apply these strategies, you'll likely find that social interactions become less about performing and more about connecting. Each step you take to enhance your social skills and manage your social anxiety adds another layer of confidence and competence, transforming your social dance from hesitant steps into a rhythm of genuine, enjoyable interactions.

Dealing with Emotional Triggers in the Workplace

In the often fast-paced and demanding workplace environment, navigating emotional triggers can feel like trying to stay calm on a bustling city street. From the sharp sting of criticism to the pressing weight of deadlines and the intricate dance of interpersonal conflicts, these triggers can significantly disrupt your emotional equilibrium, particularly if you grapple with disorganized attachment. Recognizing and managing these triggers is not just about maintaining professionalism; it's about cultivating a workspace where you can thrive, not just survive.

Criticism, whether constructive or not, can often feel like a personal attack, triggering feelings of inadequacy or defensiveness. This reaction is particularly intensified if your attachment experiences have left you sensitive to judgment or rejection. To manage this, start by identifying the specific aspects of criticism that trigger you. Is it the tone, the public setting, or the content itself? Once identified, you can employ mindfulness techniques to address your response. For example, when criticized, take a moment to breathe deeply and ground yourself in the present, reminding yourself that feedback is not a reflection of your worth but an opportunity for growth. Structured problem-solving approaches can also be beneficial here. Break down the feedback into actionable parts, assess each part for its validity, and plan your response or adjustment in a systematic way. This not only helps in managing emotional upheaval but also turns criticism into a constructive dialogue that fosters professional growth.

Building supportive relationships at work is another crucial strategy for navigating emotional triggers. These relationships can provide a sense of emotional safety, offering a buffer against the stressors of work life. Start by identifying colleagues who demonstrate empathy and understanding, and make an effort to connect with them regularly. Share your successes and challenges with them, and offer your support in return. This mutual exchange fosters a supportive network that can act as a sounding board and a source of comfort during stressful times. Additionally, consider seeking a mentor within your organization—someone who can provide guidance, support, and insight based on their own experiences. A mentor can help you deal with complex workplace dynamics and give you strategies for handling emotional triggers more effectively.

Maintaining professional boundaries is essential in creating a work environment where you can feel secure and respected. These boundaries help protect your emotional well-being by clearly defining what is acceptable in interactions with colleagues and supervisors. Establish these boundaries by communicating your needs clearly and respectfully. For example, if unplanned meetings disrupt your workflow and cause stress, request that colleagues schedule time with you in advance. If you are uncomfortable with discussing personal life at work, politely steer conversations back to professional topics. It's also essential to adhere to the boundaries set by others, as this mutual respect creates a more harmonious and cooperative workplace.

Navigating the workplace with a disorganized attachment style requires a nuanced understanding of your emotional triggers and a proactive approach to managing them. By recognizing the sources of your stress, employing techniques to mitigate their impact, fostering supportive relationships, and maintaining clear boundaries, you can create a work environment that not only acknowledges your unique needs but also supports your professional and personal growth. As you continue to apply these strategies, you'll likely find that you're able to engage with your work in a more balanced and fulfilling way, turning potential disruptions into opportunities for resilience and development.

Techniques for Impulse Control

Living with disorganized attachment, you might find that your actions sometimes bypass the usual routes of thoughtful decision-making, leading to impulsive behaviors that can disrupt your life and relationships. This impulsivity isn't a reflection of your character but more a byproduct of emotional dysregulation that stems from your attachment experiences. Understanding this connection is crucial. Impulsivity in disorganized attachment often arises as an immediate reaction to underlying feelings of fear, insecurity, or stress—emotions that are deeply embedded in the psyche from inconsistent or confusing interactions with caregivers during early development. These reactions are your mind's attempt to resolve emotional discomfort with swift actions quickly, but they often lack consideration of long-term consequences.

To manage impulsivity effectively, it's important to introduce a buffer between the impulse and the action—a moment of pause that allows you to consider the most beneficial course of action. The "pause and plan" technique is a practical method to cultivate this buffer. When you feel the urge to act impulsively, whether it's sending an angry email or making a rash purchase, pause for a moment. During this pause, take a deep breath to center yourself and think about the consequences of your action. Ask yourself, "Is this action in line with my long-term goals?" or "How might I feel about this decision tomorrow?" This momentary reflection can help you make more deliberate, thoughtful decisions.

Utilizing delay tactics further supports this process. By deliberately choosing to delay your response to an impulse, you give yourself space to evaluate the situation more rationally. Techniques such as counting slowly to ten or engaging in a brief distracting activity, like walking or squeezing a stress ball, can effectively increase the distance between impulse and action. These tactics not only reduce the immediacy of the emotional response but also decrease the likelihood of actions you might later regret. For example, if you feel the urge to confront someone emotionally, deciding to wait until you've had a chance to calm down and organize your thoughts can lead to a more constructive and calm interaction.

Incorporating long-term strategies to reduce impulsivity can also yield significant benefits. Regular physical exercise, for instance, not only improves your overall health but also enhances your brain's ability to regulate emotions, thanks to the release of stress-reducing hormones like endorphins. Meditation, too, strengthens your mindfulness skills, which can increase your awareness of impulsive thoughts and feelings as they arise, giving you a chance to choose how to respond. Additionally, engaging in cognitive-behavioral therapy (CBT) can be particularly effective. CBT can help you identify the thought patterns that lead to impulsive behaviors and provides practical strategies to change these patterns. By addressing impulsivity from multiple angles—physical, mental, and behavioral—you create a comprehensive strategy that can significantly improve your impulse control.

Implementing these techniques requires patience and persistence. Initially, you might find it challenging to notice improvements, but with consistent practice, you'll likely find that your ability to control impulsive behaviors becomes stronger, leading to more stable relationships and a greater sense of personal agency. Each time you successfully manage an impulse, you reinforce your ability to handle emotional challenges more adeptly, building confidence in your capacity to direct the course of your life more thoughtfully and deliberately.

Avoiding Relationship Sabotage: Practical Tips

In the intricate dance of relationships, sometimes our steps aren't as we intend; they may veer off into patterns that, while familiar, can disrupt the harmony and balance we yearn for. Recognizing behaviors that sabotage relationships is akin to identifying weeds in a garden; they need to be seen and understood before they can be addressed. Common sabotaging behaviors include:

- Withdrawing emotionally when things get tough.
- Offering excessive criticism instead of constructive dialogue.
- Creating drama over minor issues.

These actions, often not deliberate, can stem from deep-seated fears and insecurities associated with disorganized attachment, such as a fear of intimacy or a lingering sense of unworthiness.

Understanding the motives behind these behaviors is crucial for transformation. Often, these actions are driven by an unconscious desire to protect oneself from perceived threats of abandonment or rejection—fears that are magnified by disorganized attachment. For instance, someone might withdraw from their partner during a conflict as a preemptive action to avoid potential hurt, mirroring early experiences where closeness was associated with pain. Similarly, excessive criticism might be a misguided attempt to create distance in a relationship, driven by an underlying fear of being too vulnerable. By unpacking these behaviors and the motives behind them, you gain clarity and insight, which is the first step toward change.

Implementing relationship-enhancing practices can serve as effective antidotes to these sabotaging behaviors. Expressing appreciation actively can fortify relationships against the erosion caused by criticism and withdrawal. Make it a habit to acknowledge and verbalize what you value about your partner regularly. This practice not only fosters positive interactions but also helps in shifting your focus from what might be going wrong to what is thriving in your relationship. Engaging in shared activities is another powerful practice. Whether it's a hobby, a sport, or a project, shared activities can create fun, meaningful experiences that strengthen your bond. They provide opportunities to collaborate and support each other, reinforcing the partnership's security and depth.

Open communication about fears and needs plays a pivotal role in mitigating behaviors that sabotage relationships. Creating a safe space where both partners can express their insecurities and expectations helps prevent misunderstandings and builds trust. For example, if fear of abandonment prompts you to withdraw, discussing this fear openly with your partner can help them understand your reactions better, allowing them to offer the reassurance or space you need. This kind of transparency can transform potential conflicts into moments of deepening understanding and intimacy.

However, there are times when self-help and mutual efforts may not be enough, and professional help becomes necessary. Engaging in couples therapy or individual counseling can provide the tools and insights needed to address deeper issues contributing to sabotaging behaviors. Therapy provides a structured environment where both partners can explore their attachment styles, communication patterns, and individual histories in a way that fosters understanding and growth. For individuals, therapy can be a space to work through personal issues related to self-worth and fear of intimacy, which might be undermining their relationships.

Self-Monitoring Tools for Attachment Behaviors

The path to understanding and reshaping your attachment behaviors is not just about learning new strategies but also about consistently observing and reflecting on your own patterns. This self-monitoring is akin to setting up a personal lab where you are both the scientist and the subject, exploring the intricacies of your emotional and behavioral responses. One of the most effective tools in this personal exploration is journaling. Keeping a daily journal allows you to track your emotions, reactions, and behaviors, providing a clear record of your experiences and the contexts in which they occur. Each entry helps you to see not just the what and the how but also the why behind your actions and reactions.

Think of your journal as a map that reveals patterns you might otherwise overlook. For instance, you might notice through consistent entries that your anxiety peaks during interactions that involve decision-making with others, reflecting a deep-seated fear of making wrong choices that could lead to disapproval or conflict. By identifying this pattern, you can begin to devise strategies to manage your anxiety in decision-making scenarios, such as preparing talking points beforehand or practicing relaxation techniques during discussions. Regular journaling in this way not only enhances your self-awareness but also empowers you to take proactive steps toward change.

In addition to personal journaling, creating behavioral checklists and maintaining trigger logs are instrumental in managing disorganized attachment behaviors. These tools function as practical extensions of your journal, allowing you to systematically record and analyze specific situations that trigger unhealthy attachment behaviors. For example, a checklist might include items like "Maintain eye contact," "Express needs clearly," or "Practice active listening," with daily or weekly tick boxes to monitor how often you successfully engage in these behaviors. Similarly, a triggers log might detail instances where you felt overwhelmed, rejected, or disconnected, noting the circumstances and your responses. Over time, these records can highlight progress and pinpoint areas needing further attention, guiding your personal development efforts.

Moreover, the insights gained from self-monitoring are significantly enriched by feedback from trusted individuals. Often, our self-assessments can miss or misinterpret behaviors that others might observe more objectively. Encouraging close friends or family members to provide honest feedback about your interactions can offer new perspectives and valuable insights into your relational patterns. This feedback can be particularly enlightening when it comes to understanding how your behaviors affect others. For instance, a friend might point out that your tendency to abruptly change the subject when discussions get emotionally intense creates a sense of distance in your relationships. Equiped with this knowledge, you can focus on addressing this behavior, perhaps by practicing staying present in conversations, even when discomfort arises.

Reflective questioning is another powerful technique for enhancing self-monitoring. This involves asking yourself targeted questions that provoke deep thought about your behaviors and their motivations. After an interaction or an emotional reaction, you might ask yourself, "What need was I trying to meet through my behavior?" or "What would I do differently if faced with the same situation again?" These questions encourage you to think critically about your actions and to consider alternative behaviors that might lead to more positive outcomes. Reflective questioning not only promotes greater self-understanding but also fosters a mindful approach to daily interactions and challenges, helping you to develop healthier, more secure attachment patterns over time.

By integrating these self-monitoring tools into your daily life, you create a robust framework for observing, understanding, and improving your attachment behaviors. This ongoing self-reflection enriches your journey toward secure attachment, providing clarity and direction as you navigate the complexities of your relationships and emotional experiences. As you continue to use these tools, remember that each observation, recorded pattern, and piece of feedback is a stepping stone toward deeper self-awareness and lasting change.

Using Technology to Support Attachment Health

In today's digital age, the resources available to enhance our mental health and emotional regulation are more accessible than ever before. Various apps, online platforms, wearable technologies, and teletherapy services can play a crucial role in supporting your journey towards healthier attachment patterns. These tools are not only convenient but also offer a range of tools tailored to fit your needs and lifestyle, making it easier to integrate them into your daily routine.

Let's explore some apps first. Apps designed for emotional regulation and mindfulness can be powerful allies in managing the day-to-day challenges of disorganized attachment. For instance, apps like "Calm" and "Headspace" offer guided meditations that help you ease your stress and anxiety, enhance mindfulness, and improve sleep. These apps provide structured pathways to strengthen your mental health, offering sessions that range from beginner to advanced levels, helping you find guidance that resonates with your current state and needs. Another app, "Moodnotes," allows you to track your mood and the factors that influence it, helping you realize patterns in your emotional responses and triggers. By regularly using these techniques, you can gain greater control over your emotional landscape and learn to navigate it with more ease and less turmoil.

Online support groups and forums provide another layer of support, especially beneficial for those dealing with attachment issues. Platforms like "7 Cups of Tea" offer anonymous support from trained listeners, enabling you to discuss your feelings and experiences in a safe, non-judgmental space. Similarly, forums dedicated to mental health issues can offer insights and shared experiences from others who might be navigating similar challenges. These communities can be invaluable in reminding you that you are not alone in your struggles, providing both support and practical advice that can be applied to your own circumstances.

Wearable technology has also made remarkable progress in supporting mental health. Devices like Fitbit and Apple Watch include features that monitor heart rate variability, sleep patterns, and physical activity—all of which can provide insights into your stress and overall health. By understanding your physiological responses, you can start to correlate certain triggers with changes in your body's reactions, such as an increased heart rate during moments of anxiety. This data can be instrumental in managing stress, as it provides a tangible metric that you can monitor and aim to improve over time.

Teletherapy and online counseling have revolutionized access to professional help, making it easier for individuals to seek therapy from the comfort of their own homes. Platforms like "Talkspace" and "BetterHelp" connect you with licensed therapists through text, voice, or video calls, providing flexibility and privacy. This can be particularly advantageous if you struggle to go to in-person sessions due to logistical or personal reasons. Online therapy can be just as effective as traditional therapy, offering a real-time space for you to work through your attachment issues with a professional who can guide you toward healthier patterns and relationships.

These technological tools and services are more than just conveniences; they are bridges to better mental health and stronger, more secure attachments. By incorporating them into your daily life, you can make significant strides in understanding and managing your emotions, improving your relationships, and enhancing your overall well-being. As we continue to navigate the complexities of attachment and emotional health, these resources can serve as valuable allies, supporting you every step of the way.

In wrapping up this exploration of how technology can support your attachment health, we've seen how a combination of apps, online resources, wearable tech, and teletherapy can provide comprehensive support for managing disorganized attachment. These tools offer practical ways to enhance your emotional regulation, connect with supportive communities, monitor your physiological responses, and access professional help. As we transition from understanding these tools to applying them in everyday life, remember that each step you take with these technologies can lead to significant improvements in your journey towards a more stable and fulfilling emotional world. Let's carry forward these insights as we move into the next chapter, where we will explore deeper therapeutic strategies to address attachment issues.

Chapter 7
Advanced Strategies for Relationship Stability

Navigating the seas of a long-term relationship when you're steering with disorganized attachment can feel like being perpetually caught in fog. You long for the shore of stability and intimacy, yet the mist of past fears and fluctuating trust levels often obscure your path. This chapter is your beacon; it's about turning on the lighthouse that guides you through that fog, helping you strategize a future where your relationships are not just survived but thrived in.

Long-Term Relationship Planning with Disorganized Attachment

Imagine your relationship as a garden. Just as a garden requires regular nurturing, planning, and the flexibility to adapt to the changing seasons, so does a relationship, especially when disorganized attachment casts shadows of doubt on its soil. Setting realistic, long-term goals for your relationship is akin to planning the layout of this garden, considering what plants to grow based on the soil's condition—your unique challenges like fear of intimacy and fluctuating trust levels.

Creating a structured relationship growth plan involves more than just occasional check-ins. It's about establishing a routine that, over time, builds a rhythm of predictability and safety. This might look like scheduling weekly or bi-weekly sessions where you and your partner sit down and discuss your feelings, concerns, and pleasures within the relationship. During these times, mutual goal-setting becomes crucial. For example, suppose fear of intimacy is a recurring weed in your garden. In that case, a goal might be to share a personal fear or desire at each check-in, thus gradually cultivating a deeper intimacy.

Flexibility and adaptability in your relationship plan are just as critical as in any garden. As you and your partner grow—just as plants do—your needs will evolve. A rigid structure might stifle this growth, turning what was meant to be nurturing into something constrictive. Therefore, allowing space within your plans for adjustment and adaptation is vital. This might mean re-evaluating your mutual goals every few months or allowing each partner to express new needs without judgment, integrating these changes into your relationship's growth plan.

Professional advice, such as couples therapy or relationship coaching, can significantly reinforce the stakes and strings that support the climbing plants in your garden. A therapist or coach can provide expert insights and mediate discussions that might be too challenging to navigate alone. They can help clarify misunderstandings and offer strategies tailored to your specific attachment needs, ensuring that both partners are aligned and supported as they work toward their relationship goals. Think of them as the seasoned gardeners who have nurtured many gardens before yours—they know what pitfalls to avoid and what nutrients your relationship might be lacking.

Reflective Section

Take a moment to reflect on your current relationship goals. Are they realistic considering your attachment style? How often do you and your partner revisit these goals? Reflecting on these questions can help you gauge the current health of your relationship 'garden' and illuminate areas that might need more attention or adjustment.

By embracing these strategies, the fog of disorganized attachment begins to lift, revealing not only the path to a stable and fulfilling relationship but also the lush garden of connection you and your partner have cultivated together. As you implement these practices, observe how the landscape of your relationship transforms, how the once foggy paths become clear, and how each step you take is more confident and assured than the last.

Advanced Co-regulation Strategies for Couples

Imagine your relationship as a dance where each partner is keenly aware of the other's movements, emotions, and rhythms, navigating the dance floor with a sense of harmony and mutual understanding. This dance becomes particularly intricate when you factor in the nuances of disorganized attachment, where emotional cues can sometimes be misread or missed entirely. To enhance these dances—your daily interactions—it's vital to build upon basic co-regulation techniques and introduce more nuanced strategies such as anticipatory co-regulation. This approach involves becoming so attuned to each other's emotional states that you can respond to your partner's needs even before they escalate into distress. It's like learning to catch the subtle shift in your partner's mood by the slight change in their tone or the quiet sigh they release, allowing you to offer support right at the moment it's needed most.

Integrating co-regulation into your daily routines can transform mundane moments into opportunities for deep connection. Consider establishing morning or evening rituals that involve shared activities known to soothe or uplift you both. This could be as simple as starting each day with a cup of coffee together, where you spend a few minutes checking in with each other's emotional states, or ending the day with a brief walk, using the time to decompress and reconnect. These rituals become the pillars of your day, providing regular touchpoints that reinforce your sense of partnership and mutual support.

The power of non-verbal communication in co-regulation cannot be overstated. Often, what we cannot articulate in words is expressed more profoundly through our body language, facial expressions, or even the simple act of touch. A gentle hand on the shoulder, a warm embrace, or a reassuring smile can communicate empathy and understanding more eloquently than words. These gestures become a language of their own, one that can often bridge the gap when words fail or when disorganized attachment makes verbal communication challenging.

Handling co-regulation under stress is where the strength of your relationship is truly tested. Stressful situations can easily trigger old patterns of disorganized attachment, where fear and mistrust may overshadow the love and connection you share. In these moments, maintaining a united front becomes crucial. This means consciously choosing to stand together against external pressures rather than allowing them to wedge between you. It involves recognizing that under stress, your partner might not be their best self—and that's okay. It's about remembering that you are both on the same team, and that the stress is the adversary, not each other. Strategies like taking a timeout to cool down, using calming techniques together, or simply holding hands as a physical reminder of your connection can help maintain co-regulation even in the face of adversity.

Incorporating these advanced co-regulation strategies into your relationship requires patience, practice, and a deep commitment to each other's emotional well-being. It's about making a conscious effort every day to tune into each other's emotional frequencies, to be present and responsive to each other's needs, and to communicate love and support not just in words but through the very essence of your actions. As you continue to dance together, guided by these strategies, you'll find that the steps become smoother, the rhythm more synchronized, and the dance of your relationship a source of strength and joy in both of your lives.

Maintaining Emotional Balance in Family Dynamics

Understanding your family as a complex system where each member plays a unique role and has specific emotional needs can transform the way you interact with one another, fostering a balanced and harmonious household. This perspective is rooted in family systems theory, which sees the family as an interconnected unit that functions as a whole. Just as the health of a garden depends on the interplay of soil, water, and sunlight, the health of a family system relies on the interactions between its members. Recognizing that changes in one part of the system can ripple throughout the entire family can help you appreciate the impact of individual behaviors and the importance of emotional balance within the family.

One effective way to enhance this balance is by instituting family meetings, which serve as a structured time to communicate openly and support one another. Imagine these meetings as regular family check-ins where each member can voice their feelings, concerns, and joys. The key to these meetings is creating an environment of trust and openness, where each person feels safe to express themselves without fear of judgment. Start by setting clear guidelines that honor each person's time to speak and ensure that listening is done with respect and empathy. It can be helpful to begin each meeting with a positive focus, such as sharing one good thing that each person experienced that week and setting a constructive tone that fosters mutual support.

Managing conflicts with empathy within the family unit is crucial. Conflict is natural in any relationship, but in a family, these disagreements have a way of becoming more charged, as they often tap into deeper histories and emotional bonds. When conflicts arise, initially emphasize understanding and empathy over solutions. Encourage family members to express their feelings and try to understand the emotions behind the words. A simple yet powerful technique is to reflect back what you hear, which not only validates the speaker but also ensures that you have truly understood their perspective. By prioritizing empathy, you create a space where solutions can be found that respect everyone's feelings and needs, strengthening the family bond even through disagreements.

Role modeling emotional regulation is particularly powerful in a family setting. Children learn how to handle their emotions largely by observing the adults around them. When parents can manage their emotions healthily and demonstrate effective communication and problem-solving skills, they set a powerful example for their children. This modeling can be as simple as taking a deep breath when angry, expressing feelings in words rather than actions, or using conflict as an opportunity to teach through example how to negotiate and empathize. By consistently demonstrating these behaviors, you help to create a family culture where emotions are handled constructively, fostering a secure environment that supports the emotional growth of all family members.

Family Meeting Agenda Template

To help you implement effective family meetings, here is a simple agenda template you can adapt to fit your family's needs:

1. *Opening Round*: Each person shares something positive from their week.
2. *Discussion Time*: Discuss any specific topics or issues. Each person has an allotted time to speak without interruptions.

3. *Conflict Resolution:* If there are any conflicts, discuss them openly, encouraging empathy and understanding from all sides.
4. *Plan for the week Ahead:* Briefly discuss the coming week's plans and any coordination needed.
5. *Closing Round:* Each person says one thing they appreciated about the meeting or another family member.

This structured approach not only ensures that all voices are heard but also fosters a routine that can help reinforce stability and predictability within the family, crucial elements for those dealing with disorganized attachment.

By incorporating these strategies—embracing a family systems perspective, holding regular family meetings, managing conflicts with empathy, and role modeling emotional regulation—you can significantly enhance the emotional well-being of your family. This approach not only supports individual family members but also strengthens the family as a whole, creating a supportive network that nurtures everyone's growth and well-being. As you continue to apply these practices, observe the subtle yet profound ways in which your family dynamics evolve, becoming more resilient and harmonious in the face of both everyday challenges and complex emotional landscapes.

The Role of Forgiveness in Healing Relationships

Forgiveness in relationships is akin to healing a wound—it's a process that involves care, time, and understanding, and it's not just about saying, "I forgive you." It requires a genuine shift in emotion and perspective, which is especially complex when you're navigating the unpredictable waters of disorganized attachment. Forgiveness is often misunderstood—it's not about condoning hurtful actions or forgetting they happened. Instead, it's about releasing the grip of anger and resentment so they don't continue to poison your present interactions. It involves acknowledging the hurt and pain, understanding the context of the offender's actions, and ultimately making a conscious choice to release those feelings to move forward.

Embarking on the path to true forgiveness when you have a disorganized attachment style can feel daunting. Your experiences might make trust feel like fragile, easily shattered glass. Here, forgiveness becomes an essential yet intricate dance—balancing the need to protect yourself with the desire to open up and trust again. This delicate balance is where the healing starts. The first step in genuine forgiveness is acknowledging the hurt. This isn't about reliving the pain, but about recognizing its impact on you. The act of naming your hurt is powerful; it validates your feelings and begins the process of taking control over them instead of letting them control you.

Next, empathy plays a crucial role. Trying to see the situation from the offender's perspective can be challenging, especially if the betrayal feels deep. However, understanding doesn't mean justifying. It's about comprehending the complexities of human behavior—recognizing that people can make mistakes and that these mistakes don't necessarily define their entire being. This step can be particularly challenging for someone with a disorganized attachment style, where fear and mistrust may cloud judgment. Yet, it's a critical phase, as it paves the way for emotional distancing from the pain, helping you see the situation more objectively and less personally.

Making the conscious decision to forgive is where you reclaim power over your emotional well-being. It's deciding that you won't let past hurt dictate your future happiness. This decision might not come easily and may require repeated affirming, especially when old feelings resurface. Forgiveness is a commitment, a daily practice of choosing healing over bitterness. This part of the process is crucial for anyone, but for those with disorganized attachment, it's a step toward developing more secure relational patterns. By choosing forgiveness, you are essentially rewriting your script, learning to trust not just others but also your capacity to heal and move forward.

Moving Forward After Forgiveness

After forgiveness, the landscape of your relationships might change, and it's essential to navigate this new terrain with intention and care. Establishing new boundaries is a critical part of this process. These boundaries help define safe, respectful ways of interacting that protect both parties from repeating past grievances. They are not walls to keep people out but guidelines that foster healthy, supportive interactions. For example, if a past issue involved betrayal due to a lack of transparency, a new boundary might involve open and honest communication about specific topics.

Adapting new interaction patterns plays a significant role in this phase. It's about creating new, healthier ways of relating that don't trigger old wounds. This might involve changing certain behaviors that contributed to past conflicts or adopting new communication strategies that ensure both parties feel heard and valued. For someone with disorganized attachment, where fear of intimacy can fluctuate, these new patterns need to encourage closeness without feeling threatening. It's a delicate balance to strike, requiring ongoing communication and adjustment.

Navigating forgiveness with disorganized attachment isn't just about overcoming past hurts. It's about setting the stage for healthier, more secure relationships. Each step in the forgiveness process builds resilience and affirms your capacity for change and growth. As you implement these practices, reflect on how they reshape your interactions and feelings towards relationships. Notice the subtle shifts in your responses and the increasing moments of peace and confidence in your connections. This ongoing evolution marks your progress not just in healing past wounds but in building a future where relationships are sources of strength and joy.

Rebuilding Trust After Betrayal

When betrayal shakes the foundation of your relationship, the emotional aftershock can feel like a breach too vast to mend. Your first impulse might be to patch things up quickly, to return to normalcy. But true healing requires space, patience, and a deliberate process that respects both partners' emotional landscapes. Initially, giving yourself and your partner some space can be crucial. This isn't about creating distance, but rather about providing a necessary pause for reflection and regaining emotional equilibrium. During this time, surrounding yourself with a supportive network of friends, family, or a therapist can provide the compassionate insights and comfort needed to navigate this challenging period.

As you step into the rebuilding process, remember that restoring trust is not about quick fixes; it's a gradual restoration that demands transparency, consistency, and the rekindling of intimacy. Transparency means opening up about feelings, doubts, and fears, which can be daunting, especially when trust is fragile. However, this vulnerability is the cornerstone of rebuilding trust. It involves honest conversations where both partners can express their pain without fear of judgement, and where openness becomes the pathway to healing.

Consistency in your actions and words will be your strongest ally in regaining trust. It's about showing—not just telling—that you are committed to rebuilding the relationship. This could mean following through on promises, being punctual, and showing up for your partner both physically and emotionally, even when it's challenging. These consistent, reliable behaviors are like steady drops that wear away the stone of doubt, gradually rebuilding the trust that was eroded.

Rebuilding intimacy is perhaps the most delicate part of the process. It's about re-connecting on a deep emotional level, which requires creating new, positive experiences together to replace the painful memories of betrayal. This might involve setting aside regular times for dates or doing activities that both partners enjoy, which can reignite the joy and connection that brought you together initially. It's also about re-learning each other's emotional needs and how to meet them in a way that reassures and comforts, reaffirming a commitment to each other's happiness.

Accountability plays a pivotal role in this entire process. It's about taking responsibility for past actions and their impact on the relationship. Both partners need to engage in this accountability, not as a way of perpetuating blame but as a means of owning the parts of the relationship dynamic that each controls. Practical steps to ensure accountability include setting clear expectations and boundaries, regular check-ins about feelings and the healing process, and perhaps most importantly, being willing to admit when you're wrong or when you've backslid into old, harmful patterns. This mutual accountability fosters a climate of respect and care, where both partners feel valued and understood, paving the way for a stronger, more resilient relationship.

Evaluating the viability of your relationship post-betrayal is a critical, though often painful, part of this journey. It involves honest, sometimes hard, reflections on whether the relationship is contributing to both partners' growth and happiness. This assessment isn't just about love—it's about the practicalities of shared values, dreams, and the ability to meet each other's needs. Consider factors like whether trust can realistically be rebuilt or if the patterns leading to betrayal are likely to recur. Sometimes, despite the best efforts, the healthiest option might be to part ways, allowing for healing and growth that might not be possible together.

Navigating the aftermath of betrayal is never easy. It requires courage, commitment, and an openness to transform not just the relationship but also oneself. As you move through this process, each step taken is an act of faith—a belief in the possibility of renewal and a better future, built on the foundations of mutual respect, understanding, and a renewed commitment to nurturing the relationship you both deserve.

Sustaining Improvements: Preventing Relapse into Old Patterns

When you've worked hard to cultivate a garden of healthier relationships and personal growth, the last thing you want is for the weeds of old, unhealthy patterns to take root again. It's not just about pulling these weeds once; it's about regular maintenance to ensure they don't creep back into your life. Recognizing the early signs that indicate a slip back into old attachment patterns or relationship dynamics is crucial. These signs might be subtle, like feeling an old, familiar sense of anxiety in response to a partner's innocent comment, or more overt, such as reverting to silence instead of expressing your needs. The key lies in catching these signs early, acknowledging them without self-judgment, and addressing them with the tools you've learned.

Maintaining healthy routines plays a pivotal role in this ongoing maintenance. These routines act as both a scaffold and a safety net, supporting your emotional and relational health. For instance, regular relationship check-ins can continue to provide a forum for open communication and mutual understanding, helping to catch and address minor issues before they become larger problems. Continued therapy, whether individual or couples', can also provide a reflective space to explore deeper or recurring challenges. Just as a gardener regularly checks for signs of disease or pests, these routines help you monitor the health of your relationship garden and take proactive steps to nurture its growth.

The importance of continuous personal and relational growth cannot be overstated. In any long-term relationship, stagnation can be a breeding ground for dissatisfaction and disconnection. Engaging in individual pursuits such as hobbies, education, or personal projects can invigorate your sense of self and bring new energy into your relationships. Similarly, finding new activities to enjoy together, setting shared goals, and celebrating achievements can keep the relationship dynamic and exciting. These activities encourage both partners to keep growing—both together and as individuals—preventing the backslide into old patterns of disorganized attachment where fear and uncertainty may have once dominated.

Periodic assessments of attachment behaviors and relationship satisfaction are also invaluable in this maintenance phase. These assessments can be as formal as scheduled evaluations with a therapist or as informal as self-reflection and discussions with your partner. The goal is to honestly gauge where you are in your emotional and relational development, identify areas that need more attention, and reinforce the progress you've made. Regularly revisiting what you've learned about secure attachment behaviors and assessing how well you're integrating these behaviors into your daily life can provide both motivation and direction for continued growth.

Reflection Section

Take a moment now to think about the last few weeks in your relationship. Have there been signs of old patterns resurfacing? How have you addressed these signs? Reflect on the effectiveness of your current routines and consider what might need more attention or adjustment. This kind of regular reflection can help you stay aligned with your goals for secure attachment and relational health.

In nurturing these practices, you're not just preventing relapse; you're actively cultivating a garden of resilience and joy in your relationships. Each step you take in this maintenance phase reinforces the transformations you've achieved and furthers your growth toward a stable, fulfilling, relational life. As this chapter closes, remember that the journey of relationship maintenance is ongoing and dynamic, requiring your continuous attention and care. Keep tending to your garden with the diligence and love it deserves, and watch as it flourishes more with each passing season.

Moving forward, the next chapter will explore how to deepen and celebrate the connections you've strengthened, ensuring that your relationships not only endure but thrive in joy and mutual fulfillment.

Chapter 8

The Impact on Family and Parenting

Imagine your family as a complex tapestry woven from threads of past experiences, emotions, and deep-seated patterns. Each thread influences the design, some adding vibrant colors, while others may introduce knots that need careful unraveling. Understanding your role in this intricate design, especially when navigating the effects of disorganized attachment, can transform not only your personal interactions but also the emotional legacy you pass on to future generations.

Understanding Your Role in Family Attachment Patterns

Analyze the Transmission of Attachment Styles

Attachment styles, those intricate patterns of relating and responding to loved ones, do not arise in isolation. They are often passed down through generations, subtly woven into the fabric of family interactions and behaviors. Just as a parent's comforting embrace can become a child's first memory of safety and warmth, inconsistent or fearful responses can sow seeds of insecurity and confusion. These experiences shape a child's expectations of relationships, influencing how they will one day interact with their own children.

Reflect on the families you know, perhaps even your own. You might notice certain patterns that echo across generations, like the way conflict is handled or how affection is shown. These are not coincidences but reflect inherited attachment behaviors. Understanding this transmission can be enlightening—it offers a blueprint of not only where these patterns originated but also how they might be perpetuated or altered through generations.

Reflect on Personal Attachment History

Now, turn your gaze inward. Reflecting on your own attachment history is like carefully examining the threads that have been woven into your life's tapestry. How were you comforted as a child? What responses did your emotional displays elicit from your caregivers? Delving into these questions can be both challenging and profoundly transformative. It involves unraveling the complex emotions and behaviors tied to your earliest memories.

Consider this guided exercise: Write down your earliest memory involving emotional distress and the response it garnered from a caregiver. Reflect on how this incident might mirror aspects of your current relationships. This exercise isn't about assigning blame but understanding contexts that shaped your attachment style, providing insights that are crucial for fostering change.

Identify Repeating Patterns

Armed with a deeper understanding of your attachment history, you might start to recognize patterns in your current family dynamics that mirror those of your past. These patterns could manifest in various ways—perhaps in how you respond to your child's needs or interact with your partner during times of stress. Recognizing these patterns is the first step toward transformation. It allows you to see which behaviors are rooted in past traumas and which are informed by healthy experiences.

For instance, if you find yourself feeling disproportionately upset when your child shows independence, consider whether this reaction mirrors your experiences of seeking autonomy as a child. Such insights can be illuminating, guiding you towards more conscious, considered responses that nurture rather than unintentionally repeat cycles of disorganized attachment.

Promote Awareness and Change

The journey towards change begins with awareness. By becoming more conscious of how deeply ingrained attachment patterns influence your family dynamics, you can start making deliberate efforts to foster healthier interactions. This might mean choosing to respond to your child's distress with the comfort you might not have received or openly discussing attachment styles with your partner to navigate your relationship dynamics with greater empathy.

Embracing these changes requires patience and persistence. It involves daily decisions to respond differently and build secure attachments that perhaps weren't available to you. Each small choice can gradually reshape the attachment patterns within your family, turning cycles of disorganization into legacies of secure, understanding, and supportive relationships.

Reflective Questions

Consider these questions to deepen your understanding and application of the concepts discussed:

- What is one pattern in your family dynamics that you believe is influenced by past attachment experiences?
- How can you respond differently the next time this pattern emerges?
- What support do you need to make these changes sustainable?

Engaging with these reflective questions can help cement your understanding and motivate ongoing efforts toward healthier family dynamics. Each step forward in this reflective process is a step toward not only personal healing but also the cultivation of a nurturing and emotionally intelligent family environment.

Breaking the Cycle: Parenting with Awareness

Mindful parenting is like setting down a map in the complex journey of raising children, especially when you're navigating the challenges of a disorganized attachment style. This approach is rooted in the principles of present-moment awareness and non-judgmental acceptance of both the child's and the parent's feelings. Imagine this: each interaction with your child as a single, standalone moment, free from the shadows of past conflicts or future anxieties. In this space, both you and your child are allowed to express emotions freely without fear of judgment. This kind of environment fosters open communication and deepens the emotional connection, making it easier to understand and respond to each other's needs effectively.

One of the most empowering aspects of mindful parenting is its emphasis on emotional awareness—not just of the child's feelings but also of your own. This awareness can transform interactions with your child, particularly in moments of stress or disagreement. For instance, when a toddler has a tantrum, it's easy to react with frustration or anger. However, mindful parenting encourages you first to acknowledge your emotional response—perhaps recognizing your rising stress levels or impatience—before addressing your child's behavior. This pause to reflect can help you respond in a more measured and understanding way, modeling calm and thoughtful behavior for your child.

Teach Emotion Coaching Techniques

Emotion coaching is a technique that can profoundly impact your child's ability to understand and regulate their emotions, which is crucial for developing secure attachments. It involves guiding your child through their emotional experiences, helping them identify what they feel and why, and teaching them appropriate ways to express and manage these emotions. Begin by naming emotions as they occur, using language suited to your child's age and understanding. For example, if your child is upset because they can't have a toy, acknowledge their feelings by saying something like, "I see you're really upset about not getting to play with that toy." This acknowledgment not only validates their feelings but also helps them develop a vocabulary for their emotions.

Next, encourage your child to explore solutions or ways to cope with their feelings. This could involve taking deep breaths, counting to ten, or finding a quiet place to calm down. By consistently using emotion coaching, you help your child learn that feelings are normal and manageable, laying the foundation for emotional resilience and healthier relationships in the future.

Discuss the Role of Self-Regulation in Effective Parenting

Self-regulation in parenting is not just about controlling impulses but about being a model of emotional stability for your children. When children observe their parents managing emotions effectively, they learn to emulate these behaviors. If, for example, you demonstrate how to take a timeout when angry—perhaps by saying, "I'm feeling very upset right now and need a few minutes to calm down before we continue this conversation"—you teach your child that it's okay to take space to regain composure.

This practice of self-regulation is critical because it directly influences the emotional state of the home. A home where emotions are managed healthily is like a garden where things grow—nurtured and stable. Conversely, when emotions are poorly regulated, the home can resemble a stormy sea, where everyone is just trying to stay afloat. By prioritizing your emotional health through practices such as mindfulness, regular exercise, or even therapy, you not only improve your well-being but also enhance your effectiveness as a parent.

Encourage Proactive Communication

Proactive communication involves regular, open discussions about emotions, behaviors, and family dynamics. This might mean having weekly family meetings where everyone, including the children, gets an opportunity to express how they feel about what's happening in their lives and in the family. During these meetings, practice active listening—give your full attention, acknowledge what's being said, and respond without judgment. This kind of communication fosters an environment of trust and openness, encouraging children to come forward with their thoughts and feelings.

Adding these strategies to your parenting approach can make an impactful difference in breaking the cycle of disorganized attachment. By adopting mindful parenting, teaching emotional regulation, modeling self-regulation, and fostering open communication, you create a family environment that supports emotional growth and secure attachment. This not only benefits your children but also helps you heal and grow, making each step in parenting an opportunity for personal development and deeper connection.

Building Secure Attachments with Your Children

Secure attachment in the parent-child relationship is akin to laying a strong and resilient foundation for a house. It's about creating an environment where the child feels consistently loved, understood, and supported. This secure base fosters a child's confidence to explore the world, knowing they have a safe haven to return to. Characteristics of a securely attached relationship include:

- Responsiveness, where the parent actively meets the child's emotional and physical needs.
- Sensitivity, where the parent detects and understands the child's emotional state.
- Reliability, where the child knows they can depend on their parent for support and love consistently.

Let's visualize this through the lens of day-to-day interactions. Imagine a scenario where a young child falls and scrapes their knee. A parent demonstrating secure attachment qualities would quickly respond to the child's cries, understand the pain (sensitivity), and provide comforting reassurance that they are there to care for them (reliability). This consistent pattern of receiving care teaches the child that they can rely on their parent, building a foundation of trust and security.

Daily bonding activities are the bricks that build this foundation. Engaging in simple yet focused activities such as reading a bedtime story, playing a board game, or creating art together are more than just fun times—they are profound bonding experiences that reinforce the child's sense of security and belonging. These activities should not be about filling time but about engaging deeply with your child. For example, while reading a story, involve your child by asking them to guess what might happen next or how a character might be feeling. This not only enhances their engagement but also develops their empathy and emotional understanding.

Consistency is the mortar that holds these bricks together. It is crucial in all interactions with your child to be as consistent as possible in your responses and behaviors. Consistency in parenting fosters an environment of predictability, which is essential for developing trust. When a child knows what to expect from their parent, it reduces anxiety and confusion, making the child feel more secure. This means trying to maintain consistency in routines, rules, and expressions of affection, even when it's challenging. If you establish a rule, it is crucial to apply it consistently; if bedtime is at a certain time, sticking to it reassures your child of the structure and reliability in their world.

Handling separations and reunions is a significant aspect of building secure attachments, especially for young children. Daily separations, like drop-offs at daycare or school, can be stressful and evoke anxiety about abandonment. To ease these transitions, it's beneficial to establish a goodbye ritual, such as a special hug or a set phrase like "I'll be back to pick you up soon, just like always." These rituals become signals of reassurance that provide comfort and predictability. Upon reunion, make sure to greet your child warmly and spend a few moments reconnecting with them, discussing their day, or sharing any experiences. This warm, focused interaction reinforces that you return as promised, further strengthening their trust and security.

By nurturing these elements of secure attachment through everyday interactions, you are not just enhancing your relationship with your child but also positively influencing their future relationships. The consistency of your love, the quality of your presence, and the reliability of your support are decisive factors shaping your child's emotional world. Engaging deeply in activities, maintaining consistency in caregiving, and handling separations sensitively are all practices that contribute to a secure attachment style in your child, providing them with a robust foundation for emotional and social growth. As you continue to implement these practices, remember that each moment of connection is a step towards building a resilient and loving relationship with your child.

Healing Family Wounds

In the intricate web of family dynamics, historical grievances, and unresolved conflicts can often cast long shadows, influencing interactions and emotional climates across generations. Recognizing and addressing these past hurts is not merely about uncovering old wounds but about understanding their impact on present relationships and taking active steps toward healing. This process begins with the acknowledgment of past pains, which can be deeply entrenched and often masked by years of avoidance or superficial harmony.

Encouraging open discussions about these hurts within the family requires a delicate approach, especially when the wounds are deep and the emotions raw. One effective method is to establish a structured framework for these conversations, which I like to call 'Healing Dialogues.' These are planned discussions that provide each family member a safe space to express their feelings and experiences related to specific past events that continue to affect them. Prior to these dialogues, it's beneficial to set clear guidelines to ensure that the environment remains respectful and supportive. For example, rules might include not interrupting when someone else is speaking, refraining from blame, and focusing on expressing personal feelings rather than criticizing others. This structured approach helps prevent the escalation of emotions and promotes a more understanding and empathetic dialogue.

Facilitate Family Healing Rituals

Healing within a family can also be significantly supported by engaging in collective healing rituals. These rituals can vary widely, but they all serve to symbolize the process of coming together and repairing bonds. One powerful ritual is shared storytelling, where family members take turns recounting positive memories or difficult experiences while others listen without judgment. This can help to humanize each member's experiences and foster a deeper emotional connection among the family. Another ritual could involve writing a 'Family Forgiveness Letter,' where everyone contributes sentences expressing forgiveness, understanding, or commitment to better behavior. This letter can then be sealed and reopened at a later family gathering, serving as a poignant reminder of the family's journey toward healing and the mutual commitments made.

Incorporating professional guidance into these rituals can also be invaluable. For instance, holding family counseling sessions as part of the ritual can provide a safe and structured environment for addressing more complex issues. These sessions, facilitated by a skilled therapist, can help navigate the emotional intricacies of family dynamics and guide the family toward more effective communication and deeper mutual understanding.

Promote Forgiveness and Reconciliation

The path to forgiveness and reconciliation is perhaps one of the most challenging yet rewarding aspects of healing family wounds. Forgiveness here does not mean forgetting or condoning the hurts caused but rather releasing the hold these past grievances have on your present emotional life. It involves a conscious decision to understand the circumstances and limitations that may have led family members to act in hurtful ways. Promoting forgiveness might begin with individual reflections on what forgiveness means to each family member and their personal reasons for choosing to forgive.

Reconciliation takes this a step further by actively restoring and rebuilding relationships. It involves practical steps like setting new boundaries that respect each person's needs, regular check-ins to discuss ongoing issues, and shared activities that rebuild camaraderie and trust. It's essential to recognize that reconciliation is not always possible in every situation, and in some cases, maintaining a safe distance may be the healthiest option. However, when feasible, reconciliation can profoundly transform familial relationships, turning a history of hurt into one of understanding and mutual support.

Encourage Professional Support Where Needed

Finally, navigating the process of healing family wounds often requires more than just good intentions and personal efforts; it may necessitate professional intervention, especially when the wounds are deep or complicated by factors like mental health issues or long-standing patterns of dysfunction. Seeking family therapy or counseling can provide a structured and neutral space to address these issues with the guidance of a professional. These experts can offer strategies tailored to your family's specific needs, facilitating a more effective and lasting healing process. They can also provide individual family members with tools to manage personal triggers during family interactions, which is crucial for maintaining progress in healing.

Engaging in these healing practices requires courage and commitment, but remember, the goal is to foster a healthy environment where each member feels valued, understood, and connected. Each step taken towards addressing past hurts, engaging in healing rituals, moving towards forgiveness and reconciliation, and seeking necessary professional help is a step towards transforming your family dynamics from a source of pain to one of strength and support.

Supporting a Partner or Family Member with Disorganized Attachment

Understanding and supporting a loved one with disorganized attachment requires compassion, patience, and a deep appreciation of the complexities involved in their attachment style. Disorganized attachment can manifest as unpredictable behaviors and reactions that might seem bewildering or challenging to deal with at first. This style often stems from early relational traumas where caregivers were sources of both fear and comfort, leading to confusion and inconsistency in the individual's approach to relationships later in life.

Educating yourself and other family members about disorganized attachment is a crucial first step in fostering a supportive environment. It's important to communicate that this attachment style is not a choice but a response pattern developed early in life. Understanding this can help reduce frustration and foster empathy within the family. For instance, explaining that a loved one's withdrawal or seemingly irrational fears are not personal rejections but expressions of past trauma can shift the family's response from one of confusion or distress to one of support and understanding. This knowledge empowers the family to approach interactions more thoughtfully, reducing the likelihood of reactions that might inadvertently reinforce fears of insecurity or abandonment.

Creating a stable and predictable environment is another crucial strategy. This might involve establishing and adhering to routines that provide a sense of safety and predictability. For someone with disorganized attachment, knowing what to expect from daily interactions can help alleviate underlying anxieties about the stability of their relationships. For example, maintaining consistent mealtimes or a regular schedule for family activities can contribute significantly to a sense of order and safety. Moreover, during interactions, offering reassurances of commitment and care can counteract the deep-seated fears of abandonment often felt by individuals with this attachment style. Simple affirmations like, "I'm here for you" or "We can talk whenever you need" are powerful demonstrations of support.

Setting healthy boundaries is equally important. It involves recognizing and respecting personal limits—both your own and those of the person with disorganized attachment. This practice helps prevent relationships from becoming enmeshed, which can be overwhelming and counterproductive. It's about finding a balance where the individual feels supported but not suffocated and where other family members feel they can maintain their own emotional well-being. Discussing and agreeing on these boundaries together can help ensure that everyone's needs are met. For example, you might decide on times when it's okay to talk about emotionally charged topics and times when it's better to give each other space.

Promoting family involvement in therapeutic processes is another vital aspect of supporting a loved one with disorganized attachment. This might include participating in family therapy sessions, which can provide a safe space for addressing complex dynamics and learning healthier ways to communicate and connect. These sessions can be particularly valuable in helping the family understand the specific needs and behaviors of the person with disorganized attachment while also exploring how each family member's attachment style interacts with others. Therapy can offer practical guidance tailored to your family's unique circumstances, helping to strengthen ties and promote healing.

By implementing these strategies, you create a nurturing environment that acknowledges and accommodates the complexities of disorganized attachment. This approach not only supports the individual in their journey toward more secure attachment patterns but also enhances the overall emotional health and connectivity of the family. Remember, the goal is not to 'fix' the person but to understand them better and support them in a way that fosters security and mutual respect.

Navigating through the complexities of disorganized attachment within a family setting reveals the profound impact of empathy, understanding, and informed support. By educating yourselves about the nuances of disorganized attachment, maintaining consistent routines, setting healthy boundaries, and engaging in therapeutic processes together, you empower not only the individual affected but also strengthen the family as a whole. This chapter has provided insights and strategies to enhance your interactions and support systems, creating a more secure and nurturing environment for everyone involved. As we move forward, the journey continues to unfold with more opportunities for growth, understanding, and deeper connection.

Chapter 9

Empowering Transformation: Your Path to Secure Attachment

In this chapter, we focus on these small yet significant wins, understanding their impact, and learning how to acknowledge and celebrate each one as a crucial part of your transformative path.

Celebrating Small Wins on the Path to Security

In a world that often emphasizes grand achievements, it's easy to overlook the small victories that are foundational to profound, lasting change. Each step you take towards understanding your emotions, each moment of self-compassion, and every time you set a boundary, you are laying another block in the foundation of a more secure attachment style. Recognizing and celebrating these wins is not just about giving yourself a pat on the back—it's about reinforcing the positive changes that gradually reshape your attachment landscape.

Think of your journey toward secure attachment as a garden. Just as a gardener celebrates the first sprouts of green, acknowledging your progress, no matter how small, nurtures and grows your confidence and commitment to your path. These celebrations act as affirmations, telling your mind and heart that change is not only possible but is already happening. This reinforcement is crucial because it strengthens your resolve to continue, especially during times when progress feels slow or invisible.

To effectively recognize these wins, start by setting realistic, achievable milestones. These are not overarching goals like "completely change my attachment style" but rather measurable, manageable goals like "practice mindfulness for ten minutes a day" or "journal about my feelings twice a week." These smaller goals should be specific enough that you can clearly identify when you've achieved them, providing ample opportunity for celebration. Each small achievement is a step out of the realm of disorganized attachment and into the light of security and stability.

Psychological Impact of Celebrating Wins

The act of celebrating your achievements has a profound psychological impact. It boosts your self-esteem and enhances your self-perception, crucial factors for anyone overcoming the challenges of disorganized attachment. Each celebration reinforces your identity not just as someone striving to change but as someone who is capable of making and sustaining that change. This shift in self-perception is powerful; it transforms your narrative from one of struggle to one of strength and success.

To maintain this positive momentum, consider keeping a 'wins' journal. This dedicated space for recording your successes becomes a tangible tool for reflection and motivation. On days filled with doubt or when setbacks occur, your wins journal serves as a reminder of how far you've come, rekindling your motivation and renewing your commitment to your journey. It's a personal testament to the fact that growth is often a compilation of many small, incremental steps rather than sudden, monumental leaps.

In this approach, every effort counts, and every bit of progress is worthy of recognition. As you continue to navigate the complexities of your attachments and relationships, let this chapter serve as a reminder to pause, recognize, and celebrate the many small victories along your path. Each one is a vital part of your journey, and each one is a reason to keep moving forward with hope and determination.

Case Studies of Successful Attachment Transformations

When we hear real stories of personal transformation, they resonate with us, not just as tales of triumph but as beacons of possibility and hope. Consider the story of Mia, a young software developer whose early life was marked by frequent relocations and an unpredictable family environment. Mia's journey from disorganized to secure attachment began in her late twenties when a relationship ended abruptly, highlighting her pattern of emotional instability and fear of intimacy. Through therapy, Mia learned to identify her attachment behaviors and started practicing new relational skills. One key strategy was her commitment to "relationship check-ins" with her new partner, where they would openly discuss their feelings and needs. This gradual process transformed Mia's understanding of healthy relationships, allowing her to form deeper, more stable connections.

Then there's Jamal, who grew up in a household where emotional expression was discouraged. His breakthrough came when he attended a workshop on emotional intelligence that opened his eyes to the concept of emotional availability. He began journaling, a simple yet profound practice that helped him articulate feelings he had long suppressed. As he grew more comfortable expressing his emotions, Jamal found that his relationships, particularly with his siblings, became more genuine and satisfying. These changes did not occur overnight but were the result of consistent, mindful efforts to understand and modify his attachment style.

Each story is unique, yet common threads emerge—awareness, effort, support, and the transformative power of new understanding and behaviors. For instance, Maria, a schoolteacher from a multi-ethnic background, faced significant anxiety in social situations stemming from her disorganized attachment developed during an unpredictable childhood. Her turning point was engaging in group therapy, where she found a supportive community that understood her struggles. Through this collective journey, Maria learned to trust others and herself, gradually embracing social interactions that previously overwhelmed her. Her commitment to this supportive group played a crucial role in her growth, illustrating the profound impact of community in the healing process.

Reflecting on these diverse stories, certain lessons become clear. First, the journey to secure attachment often begins with a moment of realization—a recognition of patterns that no longer serve us. This awareness is crucial, but it is just the first step. What follows is a commitment to change, which involves both learning new skills and unlearning old behaviors. Support systems, whether therapists, support groups, or understanding partners, are invaluable. They provide not just guidance but also the relational experiences necessary for practicing and solidifying new attachment behaviors.

These narratives of transformation offer more than just hope; they provide a roadmap. They show that while the path to changing one's attachment style is undoubtedly challenging, it is also filled with moments of victory, large and small. Each step forward, each small win, is a testament to the human capacity for growth and change. As you reflect on these stories, consider how the strategies and supports that helped Mia, Jamal, and Maria might be adapted to your own life. Remember, change is possible, and like the individuals in these stories, you too have the strength and resilience to transform your attachment style and enrich your relationships.

Developing a Lifelong Attachment Health Plan

Crafting a lifelong attachment health plan is akin to drawing a map for a long, enriching voyage across oceans of self-discovery and interpersonal relationships. This map, however, isn't fixed; it's dynamic, evolving with you as you navigate through various landscapes of emotional challenges and victories. The foundation of this plan lies in understanding its crucial components, which include ongoing self-assessment, regular therapy or counseling, continuous learning, and adaptation. Each element serves as a compass point, guiding you toward maintaining and enhancing your attachment health.

Ongoing self-assessment is your navigational star, keeping you attuned to your internal state and relational dynamics. It involves regular check-ins with yourself to reflect on your emotional responses and attachment behaviors. This could be as structured as setting biweekly reviews to reflect on interactions and feelings, or it could be as informal as maintaining a mindfulness practice that helps you stay connected with your emotional state. The key is consistency; like the daily setting of the sun, regular self-checks provide a rhythm to your life that helps stabilize and anticipate changes in your emotional landscape.

Therapy or counseling, whether continuous or in phases, acts like a lighthouse, offering guidance through darker or more turbulent times. Engaging with a therapist who understands attachment issues can provide you with insights and strategies tailored specifically to your needs. This therapeutic relationship becomes a safe harbor from where you can venture out into the complexities of your relationships, knowing you have a secure base to return to for reflection and guidance. It's essential that this aspect of your plan remains flexible—intensifying sessions during periods of significant change or distress and scaling back when you feel more secure and stable.

The component of continuous learning and adaptation in your plan speaks to the inevitable changes and growth you'll experience over time. Just as a sailor must adjust sails to meet the shifting wind, you must be willing to adapt your strategies and tools to cope with new challenges and phases of your life. This might involve updating your knowledge of attachment theories, engaging with new therapeutic modalities, or simply adapting your coping strategies to align with your current emotional and relational needs. Continuous learning keeps your journey towards secure attachment vibrant and effective, preventing stagnation and encouraging the constant renewal of practices and perspectives.

Incorporating preventive strategies is essential to safeguarding your progress. Just as a seasoned captain prepares for potential storms, you should anticipate moments of regression or difficulty. Strategies for stress management, recognizing early warning signs of emotional distress, and having a clear action plan for such times are akin to having safety nets and lifebuoys. For instance, you might identify specific stressors that trigger disorganized attachment behaviors and have a plan for engaging support or using specific coping techniques when these triggers occur. This proactive approach not only mitigates the impact of potential setbacks but also empowers you with a sense of control and preparedness.

As you continue to evolve, so too should your attachment health plan. Regular review and revision of your plan are crucial. This isn't just about tweaking what doesn't work; it's about refining and enhancing what does work and adapting your plan to better fit the person you are becoming. Perhaps every six months or at the end of each year, take time to reflect deeply on your emotional growth, the challenges you've faced, and the victories you've achieved. Adjust your plan to reflect new goals, insights, and life circumstances. This process ensures that your attachment health plan remains a true reflection of your journey, tailored to your continuing growth and refined by your experiences and insights.

Navigating through life with a well-considered attachment health plan offers a profound sense of direction and purpose. It supports you in maintaining healthy, secure attachments and enriches your journey toward a fulfilling and emotionally balanced life. As you implement and refine your plan, remember that each step forward, guided by this structured yet flexible approach, is a step towards deeper self-understanding and improved relational dynamics.

The Importance of Community and Support Networks

In the vast tapestry of your life, each thread represents relationships and connections that hold the potential to either stabilize or unravel your progress toward secure attachment. Imagine each of these threads as a lifeline, sometimes becoming a strong, supportive tether, while at other times, a fragile string barely holding on. The value of a supportive community cannot be overstated—it's like having a safety net composed of numerous resilient and elastic threads, ready to catch you when the emotional ground beneath you shakes.

A supportive social network provides more than just emotional support; it offers practical help, fresh perspectives, and a sense of belonging—all critical ingredients for those seeking to heal from disorganized attachment. Such a network acts as a mirror, reflecting not only who you are but also who you can become. It challenges you, supports you, and celebrates with you, contributing significantly to your journey towards a more secure attachment style. For instance, when you share your struggles and victories with trusted friends or support groups, you receive validation and feedback that can reinforce your sense of self and promote further growth.

Building and nurturing these support networks is akin to cultivating a garden of diverse, flourishing plants. Each plant—each relationship—requires attention, care, and the right environment to thrive. Start by engaging in communities where empathy and support are the foundations. These could be therapy groups, hobby-based clubs, or online forums centered around mental health and personal development.

Actively participating in regular meetings or discussions can fortify your sense of community and belonging. Engaging with these groups provides not just support but also the opportunity to practice new relational skills in a safe environment, which is invaluable for someone working through attachment issues.

Furthermore, leveraging community resources such as workshops, seminars, and support groups can enrich your understanding and practice of forming secure attachments. Many communities and health centers offer resources that focus on teaching skills like emotional regulation, communication, and self-awareness—all crucial for developing healthier relationships. By attending these workshops, you not only gain knowledge but also connect with others who have similar goals, which can be incredibly affirming and motivating.

Sharing and Reciprocity

Active participation and reciprocity in your support networks create a dynamic of give and take that is essential for a healthy community. It's not just about what you receive from the network; it's also about what you contribute. Sharing your own experiences and offering support to others not only helps them—it also reinforces your own learning and emotional growth. This reciprocal interaction ensures that the support network remains vibrant and effective, providing value to all its members.

For example, you might share a personal challenge you've overcome, which could provide hope and strategies to someone in a similar situation. Alternatively, offering a listening ear or a word of encouragement can make an impactful difference in someone else's day, and such acts of kindness have a way of boomeranging back to you, often when you least expect but most need it. This exchange of support fosters a deep sense of community and mutual care, which can be incredibly powerful for someone working through attachment issues. It reminds you that you are not alone in your struggles and that your experiences, both challenging and successful, can serve as valuable lessons not just for you but for others as well.

In essence, the strength of your support networks can significantly influence your ability to develop and maintain secure attachments. These networks provide not just support but also practical guidance and emotional sustenance, enriching your journey toward healing and growth. As you continue to weave new threads into your life's tapestry, remember that each connection—each thread—adds strength and color to your overall picture of mental health and emotional well-being.

Embracing New Beginnings with Confidence and Hope

Each time you stand at the threshold of a new beginning, whether it's starting a new job, entering a relationship, or moving to a new city, it feels as if you're at the edge of a forest. The paths are numerous, and the terrain is unknown. Embracing these changes not as daunting uncertainties but as landscapes rich with possibilities for growth can profoundly shift your experience. These moments of transition are not just changes in your external world; they are profound opportunities to apply and strengthen your secure attachment principles. Think of them as practice fields, places where all your previous learning and efforts can be actively utilized to forge deeper connections and healthier interactions.

Approaching new situations with confidence involves a blend of self-awareness and the practical application of skills you've nurtured over time. For instance, if you're starting a new relationship, this might mean consciously communicating your needs and boundaries from the outset, reflecting the self-awareness and assertiveness you have developed. It also means engaging actively in understanding and empathizing with your partner's feelings and perspectives, applying your skills in emotional intelligence and active listening. Each new scenario is a canvas; how you choose to interact with it can either replicate old patterns of disorganized attachment or paint a new picture of secure attachment.

Maintaining an optimistic outlook during these times is crucial. Optimism isn't about wearing rose-colored glasses; it's about holding a belief in your ability to manage and thrive through changes. This mindset significantly influences your emotional responses and behaviors, shaping your experiences positively. When you view new challenges through an optimistic lens, you're more likely to engage in proactive behaviors and less likely to feel overwhelmed by setbacks. Optimism fuels resilience, empowering you to bounce back from difficulties and maintain your path toward secure attachment.

Celebrating New Roles and Relationships

As you navigate through these new chapters of your life, each role you assume, and every new relationship you forge should be celebrated as milestones. These are not just changes in your relational or social status; they are affirmations of your growth and active participation in creating a life aligned with your desires and values. For instance, embracing a new role at work or stepping into a partnership involves recognizing and appreciating how far you've come from the chaos of disorganized attachment toward the clarity of secure attachment.

Celebrating these milestones does more than just mark achievements; it reinforces your identity as someone who is continually evolving and capable of healthy relationships. It helps cement the internal narrative that past patterns no longer define you but are actively creating a present filled with growth and secure connections. Whether it's throwing a small party, having a quiet moment of reflection, or sharing your accomplishments with a support group, each celebration is a powerful reminder of your journey and your potential.

As you continue to step into new roles and navigate new relationships, remember that each beginning is not just an opportunity for external success but a profound invitation for internal growth. These moments are your practice grounds, where your deeper understanding of secure attachment influences every interaction, every decision, and every response. They are chances to live out the lessons of resilience, empathy, and self-awareness in real-time, reshaping not just your relationships but your very approach to life. Embrace these opportunities with open arms and a hopeful heart, knowing that each step forward is a step toward a more secure, fulfilled, and connected existence.

Life Beyond Fearful-Avoidant Attachment Patterns

Envision a life where the shadows of fear and avoidance no longer dictate the ebbs and flows of your relationships. Imagine stepping into each day with a sense of security and autonomy, free from the constraints that once made closeness feel threatening and independence non-negotiable. This vision isn't a distant reality reserved for the few; it's a possible future that you can start crafting today by making intentional choices and adjustments in your lifestyle and relationship goals.

The transition from fearful-avoidant attachment patterns to a more secure attachment style often necessitates thoughtful changes in various aspects of your life. Consider, for instance, the hobbies and activities you choose to engage in. Pursuing hobbies that foster a sense of accomplishment and joy can significantly bolster your self-esteem and reduce reliance on others for validation. Whether it's painting, hiking, or playing an instrument, these activities offer more than just leisure; they provide a venue for mastering skills and cultivating a sense of personal achievement and independence. Similarly, career choices that align with your values and allow for a balanced life can reinforce your sense of autonomy while providing stability and structure—key elements often missing in the lives of those with fearful-avoidant attachment.

Setting personal boundaries is another important aspect of this transformation. Boundaries help define where your limits lie and how much you are willing to engage or withdraw in certain situations. For someone with a fearful-avoidant attachment style, clear boundaries can prevent the overwhelming sense of being consumed by others' needs, which often leads to withdrawal. Learning to assertively communicate your needs and limits not only protects your emotional space but also builds respect and understanding in your relationships. It's like setting up signposts in your interactions, guiding both you and others toward more harmonious and respectful exchanges.

As you make these lifestyle adjustments, it's equally important to reflect on your long-term relationship goals. What does a fulfilling relationship look like to you? Perhaps it involves a partner who respects your independence while offering emotional closeness, or maybe it's a relationship where open communication and mutual support are the cornerstones. By identifying what you truly value and desire in relationships, you can begin to seek out or nurture these qualities in your partnerships. This proactive approach not only moves you away from the instability of fearful-avoidant patterns but also steers you towards relationships that are supportive, fulfilling, and secure.

The Role of Continual Growth and Learning

Personal growth and learning are not static processes but dynamic aspects of your life that require ongoing attention and nurturing. As you evolve, so too should your understanding of yourself and your relationships. This might mean regularly updating your knowledge about attachment theories or engaging in workshops and seminars that focus on building relationship skills. Each learning opportunity is like a stepping stone, helping you cross the river of past patterns toward the solid ground of secure attachment.

Continual learning also involves reflecting on your interactions and relationships, noting what works and what doesn't, and adjusting your approach accordingly. This reflective practice enables you to remain active and present in your growth process, ensuring that you are not passively moving through life but actively shaping your journey towards healthier attachments.

As you integrate these elements into your life—embracing new hobbies, making informed career choices, setting clear boundaries, clarifying your relationship goals, and committing to ongoing learning—you are not just moving away from fearful-avoidant attachment patterns; you are moving towards a future rich with emotional security and fulfilling relationships. Each step you take is a testament to your resilience and a commitment to living a life defined not by fear but by freedom and fulfillment.

Conclusion

As we reach the close of our shared journey in this book, I want to take a moment to reflect on the transformative path we've traversed together. From the initial understanding of disorganized attachment styles to mastering strategies for emotional regulation and navigating complex relationships, you've embarked on a profound journey of self-discovery and growth. We've explored the nuances of building secure attachments and the importance of nurturing supportive relationships, each step aimed at guiding you toward a more stable and fulfilling life.

Throughout these pages, we've delved into the core concepts essential for anyone grappling with disorganized attachment. We uncovered the mechanisms that drive our emotional responses and how they can be reshaped through self-awareness and deliberate practice. We discussed the critical role of self-compassion in healing and the transformative power of understanding and articulating our emotional needs. Most importantly, we emphasized that change is not only possible but achievable with persistence and the right tools.

I urge you to see this book not as the conclusion of your growth but as the foundation upon which you can build a more prosperous, more secure life. Continue to seek knowledge, engage with support networks, and, if necessary, seek professional guidance to aid in your journey. Remember, the path to secure attachment is not linear; it requires continuous effort and adaptation, but every step forward is a step towards a more fulfilling life.

The role of community and support networks cannot be overstressed. Whether it's through friendships that foster mutual growth, online groups that offer a platform for sharing and understanding, or professional help that provides deeper insights, remember you are not navigating this path alone. There is strength in community and comfort in shared experiences.

Now, I call on you to take that first step in applying what you've learned. Set small, achievable goals that will lead you to larger successes. Each small victory is a building block toward a more stable and joyful life. Celebrate these wins; they are markers of your progress and catalysts for further growth.

I wholeheartedly believe in your ability to evolve towards secure attachment. Remember, progress is often sprinkled with setbacks. These are not signs of failure but opportunities to learn and grow. Be patient and kind to yourself as you navigate these waters.

I encourage you to share your journey with others. Whether it's a success story or a challenge you're currently facing, your story has the power to inspire and encourage others.

In closing, remember that empowerment and hope are the keystones of this journey. With dedication, the right support, and the strategies we've explored, you are well-equipped to move toward a life characterized by secure attachments and enriching relationships. You have the tools, you have the knowledge, and most importantly, you have the strength. Here's to a future where each relationship brings joy and each challenge brings growth. Thank you for sharing this journey with me.

References

Attachment Theory: Bowlby and Ainsworth's Theory Explained. (n.d.). Verywell Mind. https://www.verywellmind.com/what-is-attachment-theory-2795337#:~:text=The%20central%20theme%20of%20attachment,to%20then%20explore%20the%20world.

Disorganized Attachment In Adults: 9 Signs + How To Heal. (n.d.). Mindbodygreen. https://www.mindbodygreen.com/articles/disorganized-attachment

Psychobiology of Attachment and Trauma—Some General Principles. (2019). National Center for Biotechnology Information. https://www.ncbi.nlm.nih.gov/pmc/articles/PMC6920243/#:~:text=Early%20adverse%20and%20traumatic%20experiences,characteristic%20features%20of%20neurobiological%20regulation.

Evidence-Based Parenting Interventions to Promote Secure

Attachment. (2016). National Center for Biotechnology Information. https://www.ncbi.nlm.nih.gov/pmc/articles/PMC4995667/

The Neuroscience of Emotion Regulation Development. (2016). National Center for Biotechnology Information. https://www.ncbi.nlm.nih.gov/pmc/articles/PMC5096655/

21 Mindfulness Exercises & Activities For Adults (+ PDF). (n.d.). Positive Psychology. https://positivepsychology.com/mindfulness-exercises-techniques-activities/

New Research Shows Mindfulness Can Reduce Impulsivity. (2024). Psychology Today. https://www.psychologytoday.com/us/blog/urban-survival/202401/new-research-shows-mindfulness-can-reduce-impulsivity#:~:text=Regular%20mindfulness%20training%20utilizes%20the,areas%20related%20to%20reactivity%20shrink.

Six relaxation techniques to reduce stress. (2020). Harvard Health Publishing. https://www.health.harvard.edu/mind-and-mood/six-relaxation-techniques-to-reduce-stress

Secure Attachment: Signs, Benefits, and How to Cultivate It. (n.d.). Verywell Mind. https://www.verywellmind.com/secure-attachment-signs-benefits-and-how-to-cultivate-it-8628802

3 tips for healing and coping with attachment trauma. (2022). Charlie Health. https://www.charliehealth.com/post/attachment-trauma

The Importance of Self Awareness in Relationships. (n.d.). Perth Counselling and Psychotherapy. https://perthcounsellingandpsychotherapy.com.au/the-importance-of-self-awareness-in-relationships/

Secure Attachment Style: Why It Matters & How to Nurture It. (n.d.). Positive Psychology. https://positivepsychology.com/secure-attachment-style/

How to Overcome Fear of Intimacy in Relationships. (n.d.). The Gottman Institute. https://www.gottman.com/blog/how-to-overcome-fear-of-intimacy-in-relationships/

Assertiveness Can Improve Your Relationships—Here's How. (2023). Verywell Mind. https://www.verywellmind.com/assertiveness-can-improve-your-relationships-7500841

6 Steps to Rebuilding Trust After Betrayal. (2022). Psychology Today. https://www.psychologytoday.com/us/blog/hope-relationships/202205/6-steps-rebuilding-trust-after-betrayal

14 Worksheets for Setting Healthy Boundaries. (n.d.). Positive Psychology. https://positivepsychology.com/healthy-boundaries-worksheets/

Can a Disorganized Attachment Style Be Overcome? (n.d.). Positive Psychology. https://positivepsychology.com/disorganized-attachment/

Online Positive Affect Journaling in the Improvement of Well-Being. (2018). National Center for Biotechnology Information. https://www.ncbi.nlm.nih.gov/pmc/articles/PMC6305886/

Mindfulness for Attachment Repair | Simple & Deep TM. (2023). Wysteria Edwards. https://www.wysteriaedwards.com/blog/mindfulness-for-attachment-repair

How To Practice Reflective Listening (With Tips and Techniques).

(n.d.). Indeed. https://www.indeed.com/career-advice/career-development/reflective-listening

Unpacking the Abandonment and Instability Schema. (n.d.). Bay Area CBT Center. https://bayareacbtcenter.com/unpacking-the-abandonment-and-instability-schema/

4 Ways to Better Manage Your Relationship Anxiety. (2023). Therapy Cincinnati. https://www.therapycincinnati.com/blog/4-ways-to-better-manage-your-relationship-anxiety

Building Self-Worth: Independence from External Validation. (n.d.). Risework Therapy. https://www.riseworktherapy.com/blog-1/building-self-worth-independence-from-external-validation

How Impulsive Behavior Hurts Your Relationships. (n.d.). ReGain. https://www.regain.us/advice/general/how-impulsive-behavior-hurts-your-relationships/

How Childhood Trauma May Affect Adult Relationships. (2021). Psych Central. https://psychcentral.com/blog/how-childhood-trauma-affects-adult-relationships

Trauma-Focused Cognitive Behavioral Therapy: Assessing Clinical Impact. (2015). National Center for Biotechnology Information. https://www.ncbi.nlm.nih.gov/pmc/articles/PMC4396183/

Why is forgiveness so important to emotional recovery from trauma and how do you get there? (n.d.). Evergreen Psychotherapy Center. https://evergreenpsychotherapycenter.com/why-is-forgiveness-so-important-to-emotional-recovery-from-trauma-and-how-do-you-get-there/

Narrative Therapy for Trauma: How Telling Your Story Can Help. (2021). Healthline. https://www.healthline.com/health/mental-health/narrative-therapy-for-trauma

How to Heal Disorganized Attachment in Adults. (n.d.). Briana MacWilliam. https://brianamacwilliam.com/heal-disorganized-attachment/

The Importance of Self-care in Mental Health. (2023). New Horizons Medical. https://newhorizonsmedical.org/2023/08/self-care-in-mental-health/

What Is a Personal Growth Plan? (Plus How to Create One). (n.d.). Indeed. https://sg.indeed.com/career-advice/career-development/personal-growth-plan

Physical health and mental health. (n.d.). Mental Health Foundation. https://www.mentalhealth.org.uk/explore-mental-health/a-z-topics/physical-health-and-mental-health

Disorganized Attachment and Personality Functioning in Adulthood. (2016). National Center for Biotechnology Information. https://www.ncbi.nlm.nih.gov/pmc/articles/PMC5026862/

Conceptualizing Emotion Regulation and Coregulation as Multilevel Processes. (2022). National Center for Biotechnology Information. https://www.ncbi.nlm.nih.gov/pmc/articles/PMC8801237/

Resilience: Build skills to endure hardship. (n.d.). Mayo Clinic. https://www.mayoclinic.org/tests-procedures/resilience-training/in-depth/resilience/art-20046311

Advances in research on attachment-related psychopathology: A meta-analytic review. (2020). National Center for Biotechnology

Information. https://www.ncbi.nlm.nih.gov/pmc/articles/PMC7451314/

Therapy For Treating Adult Attachment Disorders. (n.d.). BetterHelp. https://www.betterhelp.com/advice/attachment/types-of-therapy-for-adult-attachment-issues/

Mindfulness and Secure Attachment: Integrating Practices for Well-being. (2024). Zen Wellness Zone. https://zenwellnesszone.com/2024/04/11/mindfulness-and-secure-attachment-integrating-practices-for-well-being/

Fearful-Avoidant Attachment and Romantic Relationships. (2023). Psychology Today. https://www.psychologytoday.com/us/blog/understanding-ptsd/202307/fearful-avoidant-attachment-and-romantic-relationships

9 Science-Based Emotion Regulation Skills. (2020). Psychology Today. https://www.psychologytoday.com/us/blog/click-here-for-happiness/202011/9-science-based-emotion-regulation-skills

Introduction to children's attachment. (n.d.). NCBI Bookshelf. https://www.ncbi.nlm.nih.gov/books/NBK356196/#:~:text=A%20secure%20base%20is%20-formed,base%20(Ainsworth%2C%201993).

Can You Change Attachment Style? A Therapist Explains. (n.d.). Couples Learn. https://coupleslearn.com/change-attachment-style/

How to Build a Support System For Your Mental Health. (n.d.). MyWellbeing. https://mywellbeing.com/therapy-101/how-to-build-a-support-system

www.ingramcontent.com/pod-product-compliance
Lightning Source LLC
Chambersburg PA
CBHW030439010526
44118CB00011B/702